God Stories in America

God Stories in America

© 2017 Mal Salter

No portion of this book may be reproduced, stored in a retrieval system, or transmitted in any form or by any means electronic, mechanical, photocopy, recording, or any other, except brief quotations from this book may be printed in reviews, newsletters or sermons without the prior permission of the publisher. These stories are meant to be shared, attribution appreciated.

Compiled and Edited - Mal Salter, Sarasota, FL
Editorial review-J.P. Publications ,Greeley, Co.

Cover Photo- bay, beach, Big Island, Hawaii

ISBN 978-0-9910532-3-0

Printed in the United States of America.

10 9 8 7 6 5 4

This book is dedicated to the men and women from around our nation for sharing their remarkable God experiences with us and to the One Who orchestrated these events. Every attempt was made to keep the narrative in the original voice of the teller. Editing was for clarity, syntax and sometimes length.

Miracles

The Voice

On a dark night, no one saw the sedan careen onto the bridge, hit a concrete barrier propelling it over a railing into the Spanish Fork River 20 feet below.

The wreck remained undiscovered until about noon the next day when a fisherman saw it under the bridge and called police.

A first responder would enter the river and find the driver, a young woman, dead. She was later identified as Lynn Jennifer Groesbech, 25, a student at Provo College.

While rescuers contemplated on the shore how to remove the wreck, they heard a voice from the car say, "help."

Immediately, several men entered the frigid water and were able to push the vehicle onto its side. It was then a police officer saw a baby still strapped in her car seat.

"When I cut the straps and picked her up I saw her eyelids flutter," the officer said. A human chain, quickly formed, and handed the baby out of the river and up the bank to a waiting ambulance which rushed her to a nearby hospital. She was later airlifted to a children's hospital where she was reported to be in stable condition.

After the rescue, four first responders gathered by the river and compared notes. All agreed they heard an adult voice from the car say, "help."

"When we flipped the car (which was resting on its hood on a tree stump) onto its side, there was no one inside able to speak. "The only people were a deceased mother and an (unconscious) baby," said a police officer.

"It's a miracle," said one fire fighter, "I'm not religious but that's what you think about."

The next day, the baby's aunt Jill (Jenny's sister) reported that baby Lily was doing fine, smiling with her eyes open. She was even singing with visiting family members.

Nobody knows how the infant survived hanging upside down for about 14 hours buckled into a child's seat with her head inches from rushing water.

None of the men can explain the mysterious voice, but they all clearly heard it.

Multiple media sources
Spanish Fork, UT.

"Watch Out!"

We are driving home from lunch after church in a driving rain. As usual, I'm sitting in the back seat of our van beside our six-month- old baby, Rachel. She is strapped in her rear facing car seat and having a serious crying episode.

After several minutes of trying to comfort her, I realize that she has a very soiled diaper. No wonder she is screaming. I tell my husband, Bob, "Brace Yourself, I'm taking her out of her car seat for a minute to change her diaper."

I put her on the carpeted floor and change her diaper. I am still leaning over tying the dirty items in a Publix plastic bag when Bob yells, "WATCH OUT!"

Our van is T-boned, hit right in the back seat-drivers-side door. The impact busts out the window beside me and sends our van spinning in the middle of the intersection.

"Oh my God," we are in a wreck and Rachael is not in her car seat. Glass is raining over both of us. All I see is little Rachael in mid-air, seemingly suspended there for a moment, her bright blue eyes looking right into mine. And then whoosh…she sails out the missing window, floating like a Frisbee through the rain, across that intersection landing on her bottom in a puddle.

I am screaming, "my baby, my baby." My sweet Bob, who doesn't know Rachael has been ejected, turns around to check
on us only to find me stuck in my seat yelling and pointing across the road screaming, "Go get her, please. Go get her."

A kind man in a light blue sweater, who sees the accident, gets out of his car to help. He warns Bob not to pick her up. Try telling a daddy he can't pick up his crying baby who has just been thrown 30 feet through the air, landing in a puddle inches from the metal base of a utility pole.

Bob feels she is "whole" when he puts his hands under her to pick her up. The kind man in the blue sweater, holds a poncho from Sea World over the three of them, and walks them back to our wrecked van as I crawl over the front seat to get out.

The ambulance arrives with the EMT's who see Rachel bleeding from the mouth. They strap her on a back board and take us all to Sarasota Memorial Hospital.

Several tests are made while we wait three hours

for the storm to pass so that Bay Flight can air lift her to All Children's Hospital in St. Petersburg, Florida.

Only the patient and flight crew can go in the helicopter, so our pastors drive us to St. Pete about 40 miles North.

Rachael endures four days of MRI's, CT scans and other tests. Everyone is amazed, she has no broken bones or internal hemorrhaging. The bleeding from her mouth turned out to be nothing more than a small glass cut.

Doctors and specialist keep coming in and out of Rachel's room, refusing to accept that she is really ok. They keep telling us that when someone is thrown from a spinning vehicle the ending is always severe injury or death.

Finally everyone agrees. This is a miracle.

Bob and I are so thankful that our baby was not seriously injured. Subsequent checkups confirmed she is 100% fine.

She truly was touched by an angel.

Whenever we share her story, people cannot help but wanting to touch her. She is now a teenager and we look at every day as a true gift.

Thank you for reading Rachel's story; please pass it on. Choose to live each day to the fullest with passion. And never, never take a baby out of the car seat while the vehicle is still moving.

Dundie Crisp
Sarasota, Fl.

John's Miracle Recovery

In mid July 2009 on the island of Kauai, Hawaii, I became very sick. I had been healthy for all of my 63 years and this was a new experience for me.

After a week of high fever, aches and waking up with the sweats, I called my doctor friend in Montana. After hearing my symptoms, Dan said I needed to see a local doctor. I did and he thought it was a sinus infection. After a few days, I started getting vertigo, and having double vision. I decided if I didn't feel better in the morning I would go to the emergency room.

In the morning, I was still feeling lousy, I took a cab from where I lived outside of Koloa to the hospital on Kauai where I was admitted with what was originally thought to be pneumonia. While my lungs sounded clear, x-rays revealed two white clouds.

I was transferred by air taxi to the Staub Medical Center in Honolulu where I tested positive for Wegener's granulomatosis, a rare autoimmune disease that attacks the organs, in my case the lungs.

I do not remember much of my initial weeks in intensive care as I was drugged and in an induced coma. I was not expected to live very long and my wife and three daughters were called. When they came from Montana to visit me for the last time, I did not even know they were even there.

My body weight dropped from 167 pounds to 132. Massive doses of steroids were administered me as part of my treatment.

I had a ventilator and all sorts of tubes in my body. I was literally a rag doll and could only move the muscles in my neck. An emergency button was draped over my shoulder so I could press it by tilting my head.

I remember thinking. how am I possibly going to come back from this. I believed I couldn't and I became depressed.

The bed I was in was a special physical therapy bed which could do a wave-like motion under the body. It wasn't supposed to be on for me but it was.

The motion moved me sideways causing my body to become lodged between the mattress and the sideboard. I was being squeezed with my arms dangling helplessly over the side of the bed. Because of my awkward position, I could not move my head to press the call button. I was crying out, "nurse help…nurse help!"

Then a strange thing happened. It felt as if my spirit had left my body. I was sitting on the edge of a small stream with tall wet grass along the banks, and a mist was rising from the water. I knew if I just laid down in the wet grass it would be over. No more struggles; there would be peace. My spirit was ready to totally give up.

Then a hand gripped my shoulder. I "sprung back." I heard, "Can I help you?"

After getting help, I found out the man who touched my shoulder was the hospital chaplain. He told me that he received a call 30 minutes earlier from my friend Jim in Montana, who asked to look me up.

From that moment on I never had depression again. In fact, during the rest of my hospital stay I was even joyful. My spirit was strong and I made dramatic physical progress.

Within two weeks I was completely off the ventilator and oxygen. I still could not move a muscle but my physical therapist thought my muscles were "firing" and I believed him. He massaged my muscles and moved my limbs.

I was relocated from Intensive Care to the sixth floor of the hospital where they put patients who are recovering. I worked hard and talked and joked with almost every aide and nurse.

One day the doctors looked at me and my progress and said, "John you are a living miracle." They suggested transferring me to a nursing home in Montana where I would be near friends and my support system. The Flying Nurses International flew with me from Honolulu to Salt Lake City and onto Glacier International Airport in Kalispell, Montana.

Once back in Montana, I learned that my friends, Doctor Dan and Jim, who I knew from my appraisal business, had been meeting and praying for me every day throughout my ordeal.

You see, the doctors were right, I am a living miracle. And I was right, I could not come back on my own. I have no doubt that God, through His grace, spared my life and used my friends, care givers and that chaplain to help me. I'm still a living miracle ten years later.

John Woods
Kauai, HI and Whitefish, MT.

"Trust the Lord with all your heart and lean not on your own understanding."(Proverbs 3:5)

A Miracle for Jack

Good Friday, Jack is working out at the gym when suddenly he collapses on a weight machine and slides to the floor.

Nearby, a cardiac nurse is working out. She normally would not have been there but for a schedule change at work. Seeing Jack fall she rushes over to him and removes vomit from Jack's mouth which clears his airway passage.

When the paramedics arrive, Jack is unconscious but breathing. He is rushed to the emergency room of a nearby hospital.

In the ER, Jack remains unconscious. A couple of times the doctors can't find a pulse and he remains in a coma. The doctor tells his wife that a CAT Scan shows no brain activity and warns her that even if regains consciousness he probably will be a vegetable. Jack's youngest daughter, Colleen, a teenager, tells her mom not to believe the doctor's cryptic prognosis.

"Our God is bigger than that," she says confidently.

Later, after Jack's five other children arrive at the hospital, Colleen visits the chapel. She prays for

God's healing power for her dad. She tells the rest of the family she clearly heard a voice in her head say, "I will restore those (brain) cells on (Easter) Sunday to glorify my son's resurrection."

When she reports this revelation to her four brothers and older sister, she is met with skepticism, heads shaking in disbelief, and several sets of eyes rolling.

The next day Jack is still in a comma and on life support. Twice while talking to her dad, Colleen creates such a strong reaction on the monitoring machine that the nurses come into the room.

The second time, the nurses ask Colleen to leave the hospital room, saying she is upsetting their patient.

"You don't know my God or my dad," she tells the nurses as she leaves.

Easter morning, there is a loud banging on Colleen's bedroom door. It is her little brother announcing , "Dad woke up."

She arrives at the hospital to find her dad sitting up and being his old feisty self. A smiling Colleen joyfully exclaims, "God keeps His promises."

Jack Reilly (as told by his daughter)
Yakima WA and St. Mary's, ID.

Biker's Nightmare

We were biking through the mountains of West Virginia when we encountered hair pin curves on wet pavement. We drifted off the road and our bike spun and lunged forward.

"What's happening," I yelled, tightening my grip on Pat. "I'm trying to get us back," he screamed. We hit something and became airborne. That's all I recall

Our friends Randy and Carrie Carr, who were cycling with us since we left Cleveland for Charleston, later told us our Harley had hit a rock and catapulted into the air doing a complete somersault. Both of us fell off.

I landed in a ditch and 1,200 pounds of motorcycle landed on top of me. Randy, being a large strong man, lifted that bike off of me. He said my eyes had receded into my head and he thought I was dead.

Patrick was cut and immobile. He kept asking, "How's Julie?" They didn't want to upset him further so they replied, "She's going to be ok."

Earlier we had passed a couple on a bike towing a small trailer. It was a God thing that the gal on that bike was a nurse. When I regained consciousness she was cradling my head in her lap. She told me in a soft voice to remain calm and to be still.

Two helicopters arrived and landed on the road. They put one of us in each chopper. I remember thinking how odd, I had always wanted to fly in a helicopter but I won't be able to see anything lying flat on my aching back. I passed out again.

Hours later, I woke up in the hospital, it seems I had been given an MRI of everything except my hurting back. I was sick that night from a concussion.

It is a miracle that we both survived. Patrick had a broken T-5, T-7 vertebrae and a broken neck. When we left the hospital days later, we were quite a sight. He was in a full body brace and I was in a neck brace. I was in physical therapy for five months before an MRI was taken of my back. I had broken the same bones as my husband. I should have been in a full body brace like he was.

Today we are both walking miracles, Pat is back riding his Harley, but it is not for me. I still have back pain which I manage daily best I can, "thank you Lord."I'm grateful to God and praise him to this day for his mercy and blessings.

Julie Clarke
Charleston, WV.

Monster Tornado

May 20 is a red letter day in Moore, a suburb of
Oklahoma City. It was the afternoon of May 20,
2013 when a monster tornado plowed through this
community of 40,000 people, obliterating
everything in its mile wide, 17 mile-long path.

The vicious F5 storm contained winds of up to 200
miles an hour, This terrifying tornado tore up the
landscape, flattening homes, destroying schools and
tossing vehicles around as if they were toys.

The death toll would reach twenty four with 377
injured, most were rushed to area hospitals.

"It is amazing anyone survived this," said one
official adding, "entire neighborhoods have been
wiped clean."

The Plaza Towers Elementary School, an older
structure without an underground shelter, was
reduced to a pile of rubble with children and their
teachers still inside.

Eight children were among the dead but
miraculously many others were pulled alive by first
responders and parents who frantically dug through
the mound of debris with their hands.

Once survivors were discovered, a human chain formed passing the rescued children hand to hand to medical personnel who had setup an emergency aid station in the school parking lot.

One teacher, who was pulled from the wreckage, told a reporter at the scene that she was laying on top of five of her pupils when the furious storm hit. One boy asked, "Are we all going to die with you today?"

"None of you are going to die today," she told the children.

She said to the reporter, "Then I did something I guess I wasn't suppose to do in school, I prayed." All six survived.

Nurses at a hospital directly in the path of the tornado refused to leave an expecting mother and remained with her through the fury of the storm. Later, those nurses safely delivered the baby at another hospital, untouched by the tornado. They nicknamed the eight-pound boy, "Twister."The baby's mother had the last word and named her son, Emanuel, which means, "God with us."

Compiled from media reports.
Moore, OK.

Raging River

It is June and time for our annual family reunion camping along the banks of the Raven Fork River. Only this vacation will change the course of my life.

On the drive to Cherokee, North Carolina my wife and I talk about the offer made by the pastor of our community church. He wanted me to serve as the Interim Children's Director on a six-month trial basis.

I had served the children's ministry as a volunteer for several years while managing a restaurant for a national chain. My heart is with the children but my head and my wife are nervous about stepping out in faith saying it would be financially irresponsible to take an interim position for six months while a committee searches for a director. Besides, I would have to take a serious pay cut with a wife and two children to support.

We arrive at the campsite in a steady drizzle. Most of the families are gathered under a large tent fly. After lunch, I go fishing. The Raven River has eight-foot banks opposite the campground and is relatively shallow ranging in depth from calf deep to waist deep. I put on waders and rain gear and proceed into the calm water. Most of the adults are playing cards under the tent fly while Pete, my brother-in-law, watches me fish.

I became so engrossed in fishing that I am oblivious to what is happening around me. I fail to notice the flow of the water has increased and the river is rising.
The water changes from clear to a muddy brown and where I am standing it goes from knee deep to waist deep. Now I realize what is happening, and I turn toward the near bank. This is a big mistake.

The river is deeper on this side and my waders quickly fill with water. The extra weight drags me under like a lead sinker while the water is pushing me downstream.
I struggle to regain my footing and get to the surface, I am being propelled backwards by the rushing water.

Suddenly, I hit a rock with such force that it pops me up like a bobber. All I can do is stand there, breathing heavily, and deliberately leaning forward with the water pushing against my chest. I am unable to move.

My brother-in-law frantically yells for the other men who soon appear on the bank above me. They lower an inflated tube with a rope tied to it, but it is too short.

Next, they throw an inner tube but it blows past me and is punctured downstream when it hits a sharp rock or pointed stump. Someone finds another piece of rope and ties it to the first rope. The men lower a deflated tube tied on the longer rope into the river. After a couple of failed attempts the tube reaches me. I quickly wrapped the rope around my hand.

When the men pull on the rope, I am immediately lying prone in the water. With the river pushing me and the extra weighty waders, I nearly pull my rescuers off the bank into water.

It takes all the strength of those ten men and older boys to hold me against the current. Gradually, they ease me to the bank, which is terraced with rocks held in place by a wire mesh. I am able to grab a small tree growing out of the bank while some men gingerly crawl down the bank and help me out of the river to safety.

Later, standing on top of the embankment, several of us watch logs, branches and other debris being carried down river by the rushing water. One large log shoots right over where I had been standing helpless against the river. That could have been fatal. That day I learned the incredible power of water and how fast things can change. Pete interrupts my musings.

"Chris you have to see this," he says, holding the rope in his hands, "this is how close we came to losing you."
What had been my lifeline is so badly frayed that in one spot it is nothing more than a single strand that my brother-in-law proceeds to snap with his fingers.

On reflection, I think God was testing me that afternoon. I think about my life ending in that river. I ask myself, do I want to be remembered as a restaurant manager or do I want to be known as a teacher of God's children? I decide to take the position of Interim Director of Children's Ministry.

Chris Cahill
Pittsfield, MA.
Pastor Cahill has been serving children since 2003.

Love and Grace

Paul and "Bob"

I was going through a really difficult time. I was recovering from a divorce, my daughter was living away from home at school, and the bank I was working for was going under due to big mistakes in real estate lending.

Then the unthinkable happened. My male friend committed suicide. I never felt more alone.

The following evening my dear friend from the bank, Noreen, came to my apartment with her husband David. They gathered up a few of my things, literally carried me to their car and drove me to their home. Noreen crafted a wonderful bed for me out of the couches in her living room, made a fire in the fireplace and brought me all her frilly hankies. She also brewed my favorite tea.

While Noreen and I talked about our deceased friend, her son Paul, age 6, kept coming in and out of the room. Each trip he brought a handful of toys or stuffed animals, which he lined up next to me on the couch. The more I thanked him the more things he brought me. Eventually the couch filled. In his little boy way he was bringing everything he had to comfort his mother's friend. Lastly he brought in his most precious possession-his baby blanket. looked like a large blob of shredded rags tied together in large knots. He called his baby blanket, "Bob."

In understand all things baby blanket. Those of us who were baby blanket people have a way of finding and understanding each other. Finally, Paul and "Bob" went off to bed.

When the house was quiet, I began to cry and even sob. My grief was interrupted by the sound of shuffling little feet. It was Paul walking towards me carrying "Bob." I pretended sleep and without saying a word he gently laid "Bob in my arms. turned and left the room, closing the French doors behind him.

At that moment, I felt that God was using this child to comfort me in my time of pain and sorrow. To this day I am blown away by that precious little one obeying the prodding of the Lord and lending me his most precious possession that evening.

God graciously manifested his love that night to me.

Joy Holloway
Hartford, Ct.

Losing Battle

It was a barren season in my life as a pastor. I was so angry and hurt I was even blaming God for allowing me to wreck my life. I had sacrificed so much and he allowed this (serious depression) to happen to me.

The Elders came over with a form for me to sign that I would read the Bible every day, even if I didn't feel like it. They were young elders but it was the right thing to do.

I told them, "You can fire me now but I can't sign that form. I am not reading the Bible. I'll read the book of Ecclesiastes, it is the only book that makes any sense. I do believe in God but I'm not sure His Word is all we have made it out to be."

God heard all that and God decided, "No problem. I have lots of others ways to speak to you."

One evening my daughter Catherine asks me to read her a bedtime story. I told her to bring me a book. She returned with the Bible. I was irritated because I didn't want to read the Word, but how do you tell a child you don't want to read the Bible? I heard God's voice through the story.

That was one way God got the Word back into my heart and the other was the Diary of Ann Franck. I was watching an old version of the film in black and white, where I saw frail people fighting over crumbs. They were under the oppression of Hitler. I realized then that lost people are under the oppression of evil.

I recalled the song at my ordination, a song that I have always loved, "People Need the Lord."

I now had the answer. People need the Lord. I felt called by God to rescue the lost. They are dying and God has the solution, but I can't get to them. I felt like a gladiator who wanted to fight but was outside the ring. I remember weeping and crying and saying, "What am I going to do? I'm on the sidelines."

I called Bob Yawberg (a pastor's pastor) later that night and he said, "Jeff you are a gladiator and you will fight again but right now God is doing something in you to prepare you for the long haul. Let it happen."

I know now that it wasn't God Who was to blame for my depression. I was.

Jeff Wilson
Birmingham, AL.

A Boy Challenges God

It started like any other day for Jay, a nine-year-old, but what happened that afternoon he will not forget.

Jay was growing up in a new subdivision in Woodhaven Woods, Michigan where his dad was serving as a minister.

The homes were new and had flat back yards with no fences and all backed into a wood line fifty to seventy yards deep. It was a great place for a youngster to grow up and play. Most of the trees were hardwoods, like oak and maple, tall and straight. All except one, said Jay. That tree was forked about four feet up. One fork was badly decayed and hollow near its base, the other was solid and healthy.

Jay remembers the afternoon was very windy, lots of threatening clouds but it wasn't cold and it wasn't raining. He was standing in his yard when he challenged God. He doesn't know what prompted him. He just did. What goes through a boy's mind anyway? Jay tells it this way.

" I saw the trees swaying and said, 'Ok God. You knock over a tree and I will never doubt you again.' Within seconds there was a loud crack. Even though

I was several hundred feet away, I could see it was the forked tree that had fallen.

 "Some parents gathered around the forked tree and I went over to see. It was then I saw that the solid half of the forked tree had cracked all the way to the ground and toppled.

Surprisingly, the decayed half was still standing. You could look right threw and see light on the other side. I don't know what was holding that tree up. It looked as if it would fall at any moment.

"I thought about it. God knocked over the strong but held up the weak. You could read into that.

"The weak half of that tree didn't fall on its own. Men cut it down later so it wouldn't fall on anyone.

"I didn't tell a soul what I had said for the longest time. I guess I thought this was between God and me. Even now, decades later, I have only shared this experience with a few others for fear of being seen as bragging or worse.

"But there is no doubt in my mind that God felled the strong half of that tree that day."

Jay Hessler
Woodhaven Woods, MI.

Tender Mercies

Where would summer fun be without water? Like most kids, mine love running through sprinklers, playing with squirt guns, tossing water balloons, and yes, splashing around in a swimming pool.

Our six children were young, four could swim, while the two youngest, Brittany age three and a half and Bradley, two, could not.

Brent, my husband and I felt that with adequate safety measures in place, the purchase of an above ground swimming pool would bring all of us a lot of joy. The pool was installed along with a fence around it, complete with locking gate.

One hot sunny summer day, the kids and I were all in our backyard pool when Bradley wanted to get out. Brittany came too since I wasn't going to leave her without my supervision. Off went the floatation devises, and into the house we went.

I remember being in the family room dressing Bradley, when into my mind I heard one word and one word only. It wasn't uttered with a shout, but with deep concern. I simply heard, "Brittany."

I leapt to my feet knowing immediately where I was to go. Brittany had returned to the pool, climbed up the ladder, slipped into the water without the other children noticing, and was now completely submerged.

Leaning over the pool wall, I literally yanked her to the surface by her hair. Her eyes were wide open and her lips were beginning to turn blue.

"You couldn't see my eyes," she gasped. She was right, I couldn't.

A loving Heavenly Father could and graciously summoned a negligent mother to His little lamb's rescue. I don't know God's purpose for intervening on that day and saving my daughter from drowning, but He does.

His ways are perfect and His plan is flawless. All I can say is I am a grateful recipient of His tender mercies.

Pam Sturgill
Ashland, KY.

My Spiritual Quest

In the fall of 2005, I left my position as a prosecutor for the State of New Jersey and contemplated a trip to the southwestern US.I had started dating a nice man from the Jersey Shore and I considered moving there to start my own law practice, but first the trip. My intention was to take a journey not a vacation. I told myself and some friends that this was a spiritual quest.

I flew to Albuquerque, New Mexico, rented an SUV, and drove north towards Santa Fe. I rented a mountain bike and rode a trail high above the Rio Grande river. I rode for an hour without seeing another soul. At one point, I stopped just to listen to the silence. All I could hear was the sound of my blood whooshing in my ears.

I looked up at the blue sky with its wispy clouds. My eyes immediately fixed on a recognizable shape in the cloud directly above my head. I gasped. There was the unmistakable outline of a bearded Jesus with a crown of thorns on his head.

I was not a believer in Jesus and having been raised by secular, intelligent Jewish parents, the face of Jesus was the last thing I was searching for in my spiritual quest.

This incident stuck with me but not in any revelatory way. I thought it was a cool thing to file away in the recollection of my journey west.

When my travels took me to Moab and Zion, I had two separate encounters with Christians who witnessed to me. In Moab, I was shopping in a knick knack store which was more like a warehouse of strange things. I struck up a conversation with the owner, Robert. He offered to show me Arches National Park the next day.

We met for breakfast. I thought Robert was a bit eccentric so it didn't faze me when he mentioned Jesus on the hiking trail. I wrote a time or two, it was not to acknowledge his testimony but just to offer a thank you for a great day.

I started my first day at Zion National Park by rising early so I could take in some coffee and breakfast to fortify me for a day of hiking. It was a small restaurant and I was soon in a conversation with two young ladies seated nearby. They shared that they were both attending a Christian leadership conference of some sort. As I began to finish my coffee, one of the girls talked about Jesus being the way to salvation. I can't remember her words exactly, but her sincerity was clear as was her longing for me to understand. I finally extricated myself and walked out to my car. The girl who had shared her faith chased me into the parking lot waving a piece of paper with scripture on it.

However, despite the overt purpose of my journey being a spiritual quest, the incident with the cloud and the encounters with the Christians did not cause me to consider, even for a moment, following Jesus.

I moved to the New Jersey coast to begin my law practice. I was still dating my Catholic beau. We discussed his beliefs and he gave me books to read.

In the summer of 2006, my secretary invited me to attend a Saturday evening church where her husband was leading the music. I thought that sounded like a safe reason to go to church. When I began to attend those Saturday night services, the experiences in New Mexico and Utah returned to my mind. I was learning that God puts people and occurrences in our lives to lead us to Him.

I could not see the big picture while I was an unbelieving seeker, but as the months went by it became clear that God wanted me, specifically me, to find Him.

I now realize that Jesus is not some foreign entity, an object to be dismissed as generations of Jews have done before me. Jesus is the part of God that is observable, knowable and approachable.

I found out in August 2007, that knowing God is as simple as asking Him into my life and into my heart. It had been more than a year and a half since I began my "spiritual quest."

I had no idea then how intricately planned that trip actually had been. I had nothing to do with it. I will say on reflection that God wanted me to see that cloud the precise moment I did to see that image.

I'm grateful to Robert and the young Christian ladies for sharing their faith. I wish they could all know now that I am a follower of Christ. We may never know what seeds we sow will ripen into faith.

I thank my secretary for inviting me to attend church services and for my beau, now my husband, for sharing his belief in ways I could understand.

I now see the greater picture of how God works so specifically in each of our lives to bring us closer to knowing him. Hopefully, by reading my story, a seed is planted in your heart.

Let your real journey begin.

Alison Aaron Madsen
Brant Beach, NJ and along the Rio Grande, NM.

Father Knows Best

I grew up in a community of 2500 located between Rapid City and Sioux Falls, South Dakota.

I always dreamed of being a nurse. I even prayed to be a nurse. After high school I went directly to nursing school in Sioux Falls.

In my final year of nursing school, I received a call from a lady who was looking for an Ultra Sound technician. She said she had received my name from a friend.

I told her I wasn't interested, that I wanted to be a nurse and would finish school in a few months.

She said, "why don't you come in for a talk so you can understand what you are declining."

She sounded nice so I went and during my visit she made two statements that any soon-to-be working nineteen-year-old wants to hear.

"This position is less work and more pay."

She told me to finish nursing school and then come back and see her. That is exactly what I did.

I have been an Ultra Sound Technician for the past twenty plus years. I love what I do.

A funny thing happened during the first few years I was an Ultra Sound Tech in a hospital. I noticed that nurses take a lot of abuse. They are often yelled at or scolded by patients,
the patient's friends and family and even by sleep deprived stressed doctors.

I'm a sensitive person and when I am yelled at, I want to assume the fetal position.

I realized then that nursing would not have been a good fit for me and I would have been unhappy.

God knew all along and honored my prayer and desire to serve others in the medical field. I thank the Lord everyday for having that lady call me and explain the Ultra Sound position.

"For I know the plans I have for you, declares the Lord, plans to prosper you and not harm you, plans to give you hope and a future."(Jeremiah 29:11)

Robyn Burns Brazelton
Winner, SD.

Dee's Scary Moment

It was a beautiful October morning as Dee left Bible study at church and headed to a luncheon for widows and widowers. Dee had lost her husband two years earlier.

Everything seemed normal as she neared the stop sign at the end of the street until two teenage boys in hoodies approached her vehicle. The younger of the two tapped on her window. She lowered the driver's side window an inch or so.

"May I borrow your cell phone to call my mom," he asked?

She said, "give me her number and I'll call for you."

She dialed the number and while it was connecting she asked, "what is your mom's name?"

"A woman answered the call and I asked if she was so and so. She said yes.

"I 'm calling for your son and he wants to talk with you."

Dee passed the phone through the narrow opening to the boy's waiting hand. He turned from the vehicle and said something in a low voice.

After ninety seconds Dee said impatiently, "I have a doctor's appointment and I need to leave,"(she lied). The boy turned toward the window and seemed to be having a hard time sliding it through the narrow opening. Feeling a little guilty for her behavior Dee lowered the window. Big mistake. The older teenager reached through the window putting a handgun to hear head.

"We want your car lady. Get out of the car."

"Oh my God," I thought, "I'm a dead woman like Andrea Kruger," (who had been killed in her car west of the city a couple of weeks earlier.)

"At that moment the Spirit reminded me I had never taken my car out of gear. I slid my foot from the brake to the gas pedal, pressed hard and the car bolted forward. The boys tried to run after me but they were no match for my Honda Pilot.

"Once I was safely away I realized I was too shaken to go to my luncheon meeting. I decided to return to my church for comfort and to call the police.On the way, a truck forced me over. I was really afraid. A woman came to my car and said they had seen the whole thing and had followed the boys and called police. Later I identified the boys for the police.

 "In December I testified at the hearing for the 14 year- old who seemed remorseful. He was fined and given probation.

"In January the 15-year-old glared at me during his trial. He was put under house arrest and has to wear a bracelet. Police never found the gun.

"God was truly with me throughout all of this."

Dee Kendall
Omaha, NE.

Answers to Prayer

A Family Prayer

The Pfeiffers lived in a modest home in Hebron, Connecticut with their six children and a big dream. They wanted to operate a retreat center for anyone seeking deeper spiritual meaning,

Bill taught Latin in a nearby high school and Cindy was a youth counselor. One evening, the family sat around the kitchen table and shared what they would like in an ideal retreat center.

Bill, an ordained priest, wished for a room large enough to house a small chapel and Cindy visualized a spacious kitchen, suitable for volunteers to prepare meals.

The younger children wanted an indoor pool to swim in year round and the youngest boy wanted, "a neat robot that goes around cleaning the pool."

The oldest son wanted a hard surface tennis court and a teenage daughter said she wanted a juke box. Laughter greeted this last request but then dad added a serious note. "If we really want this kind of a center we need to make this our prayer."Bill then suggested to the children that they give something up as a family to show their seriousness in making these prayer requests. They gave up television.

The real estate market in Connecticut was in recession and the Pfeiffer television set stayed off for a year. During this time, Bill and Cindy formed a charitable organization and recruited a supporting board. After a year went by, with no television, "Then came God's answer," Bill said.

A bank foreclosed on an mansion a year ago and was anxious to unload it. The Pfeiffers drove over to take a look. A long driveway led uphill to a two-story house. Adjacent to the house was an all weather tennis court and on the other side, a carriage house large enough to serve as a chapel.

Inside the sprawling house were four bedrooms and three baths, and a large kitchen, with a commercial size stove, suitable for cooking for small groups.

The lower level had an enclosed swimming pool with a small self-propelled robot. One thing the Pfieffers hadn't prayed for was a wet bar off the pool, but in a corner stood a juke box.

Bill and Cindy Pfeiffer
Hebron, CT.

"Whatever you ask in prayer, believing, you will receive." (Matthew 21:22)

One Family's Prayer Experiences

"One time, we were going shopping , but we couldn't find our car keys. We looked and looked but we still didn't know where they were. I suggested we say a prayer to find the keys. We prayed and soon someone had an idea where we should look and there were the keys.
I am thankful for prayer." ....Vivian (age 5)

A few days after I was baptized, our family went camping at Crater Lake. When I woke up, I went running through the trees around our campsite. I realized I was missing the CTR ring Grandma Price had given me at my baptism.

CTR stands for Choose the Right. Whenever I see the ring, I am reminded to make good choices.

We looked everywhere for that ring, around the tent, in the tent, on the trails around our campsite and in the rest room. We couldn't find it. Then my Grandma Pam suggested we should pray. During the prayer, Grandma had an idea in her mind. She said we should check the men's restroom again and specifically look on the window sill. Dad and I went to the restroom. I was not tall enough to see the sill but dad could and there was the ring. We believe someone found the ring and placed it there where an adult would see it. Now I know to say prayers when I need help..Caleb (age 8)

Our family was on vacation on Maui at our favorite baby beach, when a woman approached and asked if we had lost anything. I looked around quickly and I told her I didn't think so.

Back in our condo, we realized our GoPro, underwater camera, was missing. Jordan returned to the beach to look for the camera and the woman. He returned empty-handed.

We posted the lost camera on Craigslist. That evening we received a call that our camera had been found. The caller was the woman on the beach. The next day we gratefully received the camera and the photos saved on it. We are grateful to have had these prayer experiences as a family. Our children still talk about them.

Jordan and Shana Price and Children
Portland, OR.

Tebow and *Shaken*

Christmas week and I wake up praying about what to get my husband Paul. I hear in my head, "Tebow and Shaken." I have learned to act on promptings from the Lord.

Paul is a fan of Tim Tebow, the Heisman Trophy winning quarterback who led Florida to the National Football Championship in 2009, and especially because he is vocal about his Christian faith.

I drive to the Life Way Christian Book store in search of Tebow's latest best seller, *"Shaken."* After not finding the book, I ask a clerk for help.

"I'm sorry," the clerk says apologetically, "we sold out and that title is on back order."

Kathy heads off to another store immediately and goes to the book section only to be disappointed again. This store, the manager tells her, doesn't carry that book but he will be glad to order it. The book should be here in a week to ten business days, he says. That won't work with Christmas days away.

Frustrated and confused, Kathy begins to wonder why would she be prompted to purchase *"Shaken"* and not be able to find the book.

She calls a friend, tells her about the challenge to find a copy of *"Shaken."* Kathy asks, "Is there another Christian book store in the area?"

"Have you tried The Bible store?" her friend asks.

Kathy goes to the Bible Store and begins a frantic search. No Luck. She is standing there in the aisle feeling shaken herself. She is puzzled why she can't find the book when she clearly heard the words Tebow and *Shaken* when she prayed.

She is startled when she hears in her head, "Turn Around." She does and facing her is a single copy of *"Shaken"* in the back of a shelf.

"I immediately grab it with both hands and holding it out in front of me, I march directly to the checkout counter."

The clerk says, "I thought we had sold our last copy."

"No," I said, holding tightly onto the book, "this is the last copy. Praise the Lord."

Kathy Boiano
Jackman, ME and Charlotte, NC.

Hope Haulers

I'm a salesman and a part time chaplain to the trucking industry. This is a true story.

Three days after September 11, 2001 I was on my way to Destin Florida for the annual convention of the Tennessee Trucking Association where I planned to launch Hope Haulers, a family of services to and through the trucking industry. Upon arrival I wasn't surprised to find everyone talking about 9/11. When I spoke with the association president, he asked me if I would deliver the opening prayer.

When I stood up in front of the convention, not having planned this, I said, "looking out at your faces I see some of you are wondering what is going on in the world and others of you look worried. I might feel the same way if it were not for my faith and knowing my destiny. I believe God has us all here for a reason and if any of you have uncertainty in your life and are anxious, see me before you leave this conference."

Two hundred and fifty people came up to talk with me over the next three days.Shortly after returning to Nashville, I went to the chapel at the truck stop in

Antioch to pick up some tools I had left and to talk with Chaplain Doug.

A young man came in and started asking the chaplain questions. The nature of the questions told me I should retreat to the chaplain's quarters and pray for Doug while he talks with the man. I could hear the chaplain making progress when a lady truck driver came in and interrupts the conversation. I came out and suggested that she and I go next door to the restaurant. She is angry with God and unloads on me. We talked for more than an hour before she calmed down. I realized I had to leave. I gave her my cell number and headed back to the chapel to pickup my tools.

The chapel was empty and I wondered how Doug made out with the young man. As I walked out of the chapel with my tools, I noticed a truck waiting to pull up to the fuel isle but there was no truck in front of it. The driver was just staring ahead.

I yelled, "hey trucker, you can move up." No response, the driver continued looking ahead.

I walked over and jumped up on his rail. "You ok?"

The driver slowly moved his head and said he was waiting for his wife who was in the restaurant and added, "I'm a mess." I told him to pull around and park and meet me in the chapel. I dropped my tools off in my truck.

I spotted Doug in the restaurant. He told me he had a good talk with the young man and has scheduled a follow up tomorrow. Together we went into the chapel and prayed for the man parking the truck.

After a few minutes, that man came into the chapel.

"You have something heavy weighing you down?"

He nodded. I asked, "Are you a Christian?"

He replied, "Sorta."

"Let's address sorta. What do you mean by sorta?"

He tells me that he was kicked out of his house when he was 15, moved into the home of a pastor and his wife. He lived in the basement for two years and that is when he, "sorta," heard about the Lord.

"I find a good starting point is getting right with the Lord. Would you like to do that?"

"OK, how do I do that?"
"Go for it! Just start praying."

After a long silence he started to sweat.

I said, "Tracey there is a battle going on right now over you. If it is alright with you, I'm going to put my hands on you and I'll pray over your body. Are you comfortable with this?" He nodded OK.

After two minutes of prayer he opened up and out came a stream of confession, repentance and acceptance of Jesus as his Lord and Savior. We all rejoice. He told us that the gal waiting for him was not his wife but his live-in girlfriend.

"I need to get right with her. He looked at me and said, "When I saw you go into the chapel I wondered if you were the chaplain. When I saw you come out I hoped you would come over. When you spoke, I couldn't move my head was like frozen.

"I'm an owner operator. I've lost my job, I'm broke. I had a spot picked out, one and half hours up the road. where I was going to drive off and end it all.

"Then you jumped up on my truck."

Chuck Sonn
Nashville, TN.

The Lost Wallet

Jim lost his wallet and that affected the whole family. He didn't realize he had misplaced his wallet until he was getting ready Sunday night and preparing for the morning commute.

He had washed two cars and detailed them Sunday afternoon so that was the first two places he looked.

The children and I started the search inside the house, starting with the obvious like the nightstand by the bed and the buffet in the dining room. We progressed to feeling in the crevasses of the cushions on the couch and inside the levels of the Lazy Boy chair. Soon we were trashing the house. All was for naught.

Monday morning Jim drove off to work without his wallet and of course without his license. I prayed the wallet would be found. Monday night we resumed the search perhaps more frantically than the day before.

Jim and the kids went out and checked the cars again, while I looked around inside revisiting many of the same places I had searched before. No wallet. I prayed some more.

Tuesday, Jim was obviously still upset and began grumbling about the prospect of having to apply for a duplicate license and calling the credit card companies to close the accounts.

As he stood by the door, he said he was going to take my car this morning because the SUV was low on gas. I suggested we pray together, something we hadn't done for awhile. So we did.

We didn't ask that the wallet be found but we praised the Lord for all that we did have, confessing that we didn't have to worry about these things but give it all over to Him. I felt better after praying.

I walked Jim out to my car. As he opened the door he shouted, "There's my wallet!"

I took a step forward and I saw it too. His wallet was on the floor in front of the back seat, in plain sight. He and the kids had searched both vehicles twice, as recently as last night. That wallet could not have been out in the open like that.

How did it get there? What if he hadn't decided to take my car instead of his today? What if we hadn't prayed as we did? Thank you Lord.

Cathy Pansa
Shorewood, IL.

"God Give Me A Sign"

"Some of you are feeling pretty low right now but believe me you will feel a lot better in twelve weeks."

I heard him loud and clear. I wanted this 12-week Divorce Recovery Workshop at my church to be over now so I could feel better. The instructor was right about one thing. I was feeling lower than a reptile slithering in the mud. I hoped he was right about feeling better. All I could do now was hold onto that hope.

My marriage of seven years wasn't officially over yet, but it had ended a long time ago. Drugs and alcohol had taken a toll. I had been the one to sober up first but all I got for my effort was verbal abuse from a husband that blamed everything on me.

He continued to medicate himself while I felt a constant ache of loneliness and the pain from the yelling and nightly name calling. There seemed to be no end. Somebody had to end this madness. I moved out and filed for divorce.

I told all this to my Divorce Recovery small group. Each person in the group was encouraged to share their situation. We all listened to each other with sympathy and compassion. I felt particularly sorry for the gals with young children. At least I didn't have that problem.

A childhood disease had left me barren. I didn't think I could ever feel good about that, but I was thankful now that I didn't have to go through this with a child too.

The group and our facilitator became my support base for the next several weeks. We helped each other deal with the grieving over the loss of an intimate relationship and to focus on what we had to do to become a whole person again. That meant we had to let go of the anger and the blame in order to begin the healing process.

The group was there for me the night my divorce became official by court order. I was glad to be with them and not alone in my apartment.

The instructor was right. I did feel better on "graduation night" from the workshop, and there were plenty of tears and hugs and brownies. Our group exchanged phone numbers before leaving.

The high I felt at the end of the workshop came crashing down a week later when I lost my high salaried marketing position. The corporation just eliminated the entire department.

I was devastated. During all the trials of the divorce I had poured myself into the job and had relied on the steady income to keep me independent. Now what would I do once the severance pay ran out?

I went into depression. It got worse as the weeks went by and I couldn't find another position within the corporation or a like paying job in the city.

I was at or nearing the bottom of my depression pit when a friend from the divorce group called. She asked me how I was doing and I told her. She invited me to her son's sixth birthday party that afternoon and I at first declined. But she insisted and I thought maybe it would cheer me up.

The party was outside in the yard. It was a mistake to be there. The children playing and the mother's talking about kids and families depressed me more. When they were occupied with a pin the tail on the donkey game, I slipped into the house.

I wandered into the living room and all of a sudden the tears gushed out. I was shaking. I cried out to the Lord. With my head bowed and with my hand gripping the fireplace mantle, I said, "Lord are you there? Let me know. Give me a sign that you hear me, that I matter."

My tears subsided and the shakes stopped. I lifted my head slowly and there in front of me above the mantle, I saw through moist eyes a framed copy of "Footprints."

Mary Beth Darling
Las Vegas, NV.

Family Vacation

When was the last time you had a week- long family vacation?

We have had family gatherings before especially around the holidays for a meal or two; but we hadn't all been together for a week in more in twenty years. My three grand children have grown since then and now have a child of their own. Through a second marriage, I inherited a daughter and son-in law and now two additional granddaughters.

My wife, Joy, and I had permanently moved from New England to Florida while our blended family lives in Connecticut, Massachusetts and Pennsylvania, making for limited visits. I was feeling a disconnect with our family. It was time for all of us to get together for a week. I put it on my bucket list.

I began praying about it in March. When I broached the idea to family members in April there was an immediate positive response. Trying to coordinate schedules among six families was a challenge. We collectively decided on the third week of August before schools restarted.

We selected a private Delaware beach where my oldest daughter owned a cottage which could sleep 6 to8. I rented a large beach house nearby which could accommodate ten. This was perfect, because there would be 18 of us including my ex and her partner (Yes! After all, she is part of the family and praise God, she and my wife get along fine.)

Each family unit had to drive hundreds of miles to get there. One family rented a van to take more people and luggage with them and another family member stayed back in Massachusetts with two dogs and a cat as two people had pet allergies.

The rest arrived as scheduled, full of excitement and anticipation of a fun filled vacation with each other. We had agreed in advance that people could do what they wanted each day but we would all gather every evening for dinner. Each family unit was assigned with providing one of the evening meals.

The Lord provided a perfect week of beach weather and it was a delight to see adults and the children frolicking together on the sand and in the water. The days were filled with sunshine, laughter and love. Our ages ranged from 15 months to 82 years. The older ones served the younger ones and the adults served everyone and each other. I think the heaviest object I lifted all week was a cup of coffee made by someone else.

Joy and I, both believers, agreed to model our faith but not be evangelists. We offered a prayer before the evening meal and loved on everybody.

On Wednesday evening, we all gathered on the beach around a fire. There was a water balloon fight and the children toasted marsh mellows to make S'mores. We said goodbye to two family units who were leaving the next day for previous commitments. It was a moment of reflections and sharing. We even sang one verse of "Kumbaya My Lord."

The next day, the dog sitter arrived and we finished out the week with fellowship, laughter and fun. We all departed knowing we had a very special time together.

The next week, one of my adult granddaughters posted on her Facebook; "On reflection it was the best family vacation I have ever had. Waking up under the same roof with my dad, brother and sister in more than ten years...seeing our children playing and laughing endlessly, watching both sets of my grandparents at the same table playing with their great grand children...and cherishing making new memories and laughing about the old ones. You can't put a price tag on those moments. This vacation was everything I didn't know I needed."

Lots of likes were checked on her reflection.

I praise the Lord for blessing us all and for answering a great grandfather's prayer request. It was beyond my expectations. Our Lord often responds that way.

We have a God that loves loving families.

When is your next family vacation?

Invite God along and keep praying.

Mal Salter
Broadkill Beach, DE.

Angels

Andrew's Visitor

My son Andrew was playing tee-ball and I was
coaching third base. My eight- year old hit a nice
blooper into right field. As he rounded the base I
could see something was wrong.

One of his team mates called out to me and said,
"Andrew is crying"! I ran to my son and he told me
he was feeling sick to his stomach. I excused us and
headed home.

For the next few days Andrew couldn't keep
anything down and he was miserable. His
pediatrician looked him over and said he had the flu
and to keep him hydrated as much as possible. After
a couple of days his condition hadn't improved so
we took Andrew to the local hospital. They kept
him for two days and said there wasn't anything
else they could do for him and sent him home.

The following morning when Andrew woke up his
eyes were crossed and his speech was slurred. His
mother called the ER at All Children's Hospital in
St. Petersburg and they suggested we bring him in

immediately. For two days, they performed all sorts of tests and determined that Andrew had a stroke.

Over the next four months our son underwent a myriad of tests and procedures. Dozens of doctors checked in on him, scanning his chart, and asking a laundry list of questions, but to this day, we still do not know what caused the stroke.

While Andrew was in the hospital, my routine was to work until two or three in the afternoon before heading toSt. Petersburg to be with him. At 10:00 pm I would drive home and start the process again the next day.
One day, I had just arrived at home when the phone rang. It was Andrew's mother who hadn't left his side since this ordeal began. She told me that Andrew was having trouble breathing and that they were moving him into ICU.

I immediately wanted to jump back in my car and return to the hospital, but I was exhausted and decided to get a couple hours of sleep.

I arose the next morning at five and grabbed a quick shower. During the 45 minute drive to St. Petersburg I had a continuous conversation with God. My prayer went from pleading to yelling to negotiating with Him. "Why are You doing this to my son? He's only eight! Please heal him!"

When I arrived it was 6:30 A.M., I rushed into ICU where Andrew lay in a bed with wires attached to his chest and an oxygen cannula wrapped around his head. Being sensitive to sound and light he had a wash cloth draped over his eyes. I bent over and kissed his head and whispered, "Dad is here." His mother stood on the other side of the bed and looked like she hadn't slept much.

At 7:00, a nurse came into the room and told us we had to leave for an hour while they transitioned to the next shift. We both walked silently out, deep in thought, hoping the hour would pass quickly.

In the waiting room I saw a familiar face. It was an elderly man from my church who came to be with me and offer support. I filled him in on Andrew's condition and we prayed for mercy.
He took a dog-eared piece of yellowed paper out of his wallet and began to read it to me. The article talked about dealing with adversity but all I remember is the phrase, "God is sovereign."
When the ICU was open again, I thanked my visitor and rushed back to Andrew's room. Again, his mother and I stood on either side of the bed and just watched our son fight off the pain. A few minutes went by when the door opened and a tall man walked into the room.

"Is this Andrew Bartlein?" We both nodded.

The man explained that a local church had told him about Andrew and asked him to visit. Neither Andrew's mother nor I recognized the name of the church. He went on to tell us about his daughter who was born with Cystic Fibrosis and that he understood what we were going through. He said it all came down to this, "God is sovereign." I couldn't believe my ears and before I could say anything he asked if he could pray for Andrew's healing. Again, we nodded and joined hands.

The stranger offered a moving and inspiring prayer for the restoration of our son. His mom and I held Andrew's hand while the man prayed. At the end of the prayer, Andrew lifted the wash cloth from his eyes and said, "Amen!"

While we were focused on Andrew, the man slipped out of the room quietly. We never saw him again.

Today, Andrew is 26, married and has completed two years of Bible college and although he still has complications due to the stroke, he does not let that get in the way of serving God. Occasionally, he'll say something about his experience, but whenever he tells this story he talks about the angel that came to visit and prayed over him.

Randy Bartlein
Brookfield, WI and St. Petersburgh, Fl.

A Toddler and a Stranger

My husband and I had been attending the Church of the Way in Van Nuys, California for some time.

This particular Sunday was baby dedication day but our 15 month old stayed in the nursery because we had had her dedicated earlier. Following the brief ceremony the parents returned their babies to the nursery.

Looking back, we think that was when a door must have been left open and our little Andrea slipped out of the nursery unnoticed.

She apparently made her way outside to the sidewalk and walked between two parked cars. She was about to enter busy Van Nuys Boulevard when a man picked her up and brought her into the church foyer.

He presented her to an elder, saying simply, he found this little girl getting ready to cross Van Nuys Boulevard. The elder recognized Andrea and sent someone to get me.

When I saw Andrea, she was lying quietly in the arms of the elder. It wasn't until she saw me that she began to scream.

Together, the three of us went back to the nursery. Everyone there was upset that Andrea had gotten out and relieved that she was safe.

The man who brought her in was gone and the elder said he hadn't seen him before. The odd thing was Andrea didn't go to men, not even to her dad. Her tendency would be to run from a man, especially a stranger.

But the elder said she looked very peaceful in the man's arms, and she didn't fuss when he took her from him and cradled her.

Some may call this luck but after people had calmed down the sentiment at the nursery was that someone was looking out for Andrea and sent an angel to rescue my little girl.

I would not argue otherwise.

Barbara Koukl
Van Nuys, CA.

Christmas Headwinds

I had a break in my residency at Walter Reed Army Medical Center in Washington, DC, and I was looking forward to spending Christmas with my family in Phoenix.

When I arrived at the airport, I discovered that my flight had been canceled because of weather. Like hundreds of other disappointed travelers, I stood in line to get help getting out of Washington, DC.

My hope faded when the airline attendant behind the counter looked like a teenager filling in during his holiday break. When I explained my situation, he quickly suggested an alternate flight that was leaving for Pittsburgh and from there to LA.

I said something about my destination being Phoenix. He explained that the LA flight would have to refuel in Phoenix due to headwinds and I could get off there.

In Pittsburgh I told the flight attendant my situation and she said she would inform the crew. While waiting to take off, the pilot came on the intercom and announced, "would the guy who thinks he is going to Phoenix please come forward."

All eyes were on me as I walked forward. Everybody was having a good laugh at my expense.

The crew was adamant. They were not stopping in Phoenix but I could go to LA and then catch a flight back to Phoenix. I agreed to do this and returned to my seat in the main cabin.

Everyone settled down for a smooth flight. Well into the night, the captain made an apology for disturbing us. He announced he had good news for one passenger and bad news for everybody else. Because of headwinds, they were low on fuel so we were stopping in Phoenix to refuel. I wanted to gloat but held it to a smug grin.

We landed in Phoenix and parked on the tarmac. The rear staircase was lowered and I was taken to the terminal in a service truck.

I never found a logical explanation for how the young counter worker in Washington knew the plane would have to refuel in Phoenix when the flight crew was so certain it would not.

Was the agent an angel? I guess I'll never know. After all it was Christmas.

Gerald Knighton
Phoenix, AZ and Washington, DC.

I Was a Stranger

I was a stranger in a strange land. I was lost, tired and alone. I thought of giving up until something happened that I don't fully understand to this day.

Having attended college close to home, I was venturing into a seminary that was across the country. My father drove me to the Atlanta airport at five A.M. for a flight to San Francisco with a short layover in Dallas. Once in San Francisco, a representative from the seminary was to meet me and take me to my new home. You know, "The Devil is in the details."

A thick fog settled over Dallas. Scores of planes, including ours, were rerouted to Lubbock Texas, which was totally unprepared for the role now thrust upon it. Chaos reigned. I sat in the Lubbock airport for eight hours. My five hour trip became15 hours.

By the time I arrived, the seminary representative was long gone. There I was in the airport feeling lost. My food intake for that day could be measured in peanuts. I began contemplating taking a flight back to Atlanta when I heard an announcement calling my name. I went to the desk and the agent said, "That woman over there is looking for you." She was a kind looking woman in her early fifties. I said, "I'm Paul Kerbas."

"Oh Paul," she said, "you must be so tired. What a journey you have been on and your luggage isn't coming until much later tonight. My husband and I live nearby. Come to our house, eat dinner and rest and I will bring you back to the airport later.

Surprised, I asked, "How did you know about me?"

She said, "Paul, one thing you will learn is that here at the seminary we are a caring community."

We drove to her house, I enjoyed a hot meal before going into her guest room where I fell asleep. Around 11p. m. she drove me to the airport and my luggage was there. She set me on the right bus and told me what stop to get off at. Then just as quickly as she had entered my life, she disappeared.

Now, twenty years later, I can't tell you anything more about that woman. Despite my efforts. I could not trace her at all. No one in the seminary could tell me her name and she remains a mystery. I am left to wonder if she was a kind hearted soul who reached out to me or is it possible that on my bumpy road to seminary an angel paved the way?

Paul Kerbas
Lubbock, TX and San Francisco, CA.

Growing up in Rural Iowa

In 1951, Mt. Pleasant was a small town of about 6,000 in Southeastern, Iowa. It was the county seat of Henry County, serving the outlying farming community. It was a great place to grow up.

Our group consisted of my brother Duane, Arden, Don, Will and myself. We all lived near each other and Duane and Arden were a year older than the rest of us.

When we wanted to play pool we had to drive 15 miles east to New London. We liked the pool hall because it was smoky and we could use it as an excuse when we came home smelling smoky, "Yep, been down shooting pool in New London."

During the winter months we usually had packed snow on the streets because Mt. Pleasant didn't have snowplows. When that happened, we'd crouch behind a car that had stopped for a stop sign and grab the rear bumper. We could slide on our shoes very easily. The only problem was you had to be careful when the car crossed the railroad tracks because your shoes could catch on the rails and send you rolling. We'd ride all over town this way, changing directions with different cars.

One nice snowy evening, Don was just leaving for his girl friend's house, the three of us hopped on the rear bumper. When Don found it was hard to gain speed he realized he had hoppers on the back. He cut a corner sharp to throw us off. The car spun around and the rear tire hit the curb, sending the three of us flying. Sadly for Don, the car kept sliding until the rear fender hit a post. Big Dent.

Duane and I were in seventh and eighth grade when our parents went on a trip. The next thing we knew there was a poker game in our kitchen organized by our older brother, Elwood. We thought this was what you did when your parents went out of town. So that's what we did when we were in high school.

Whenever our parents left, within a few minutes our friends would show up and stay for as long as our parents were gone.

One year they went to California for a month. Arden set a record of 30 days at our house. Usually every bed was occupied and many evenings we played poker or black jack most of the night.

The people that traveled with our parents to California left their car with us. Of course, I didn't want the battery to go dead so I drove it to school every day. It was a 1951 Pontiac, a nice car! We started driving around town late at night playing

"Ditch'em." One car would be the hare and the second car the hound, and the chase was on.

Near the end of the extended California trip, the house was getting messy. The sink was full of dishes, some had been there 28 days, cigarette butts in bags and lots of trash. (Note: no beer cans, we didn't drink. We had some standards.)
The next day we came home to find the house clean, ashtrays emptied, dishes washed and put away. We were in shock. Who did this?

It had to be some of the ladies from church who knew our folks were gone. We didn't say anything to anyone and whoever cleaned up the house didn't either. Whoever it was, thank you for cleaning and for keeping your mouth shut.

Since our father was a Methodist minister, I think Duane and I felt we had to prove that we were no different than the other kids. Being a PK (preacher's kid) is a tough mantel to overcome. I don't think our friends ever thought about it, but adults saw us differently.

When Elwood, the captain of the Atlantic High School football team, was caught along with his teammates stealing watermelons, the cops said, "we can't arrest the preacher's kid," so they let him go.

We never heard all the tales about Elwood. He was always circumspect but we knew he always had something going on.

Recently I told his wife, that if Elwood's early history had ever come to light, he never would have been appointed to the Missouri Supreme Court. Duane and I were proud of our brother and tried to emulate him.

Recalling what we did growing up some six decades ago, I now realize our hometown was appropriately named and I sense someone was looking over us.

Being a Preacher's Kid, I know who.

Excerpted from **Memories** *of the way we were*

Melvin L. Thomas
Mt. Pleasant, IA.

" God will command His angels concerning you to guard you in all your ways." (Psalm 91:11)

Family Mystery

It is one of those unexplained events in our family. Grandfather came from his house on the Rhode Island shore to spend the better part of the week helping my dad replace the front porch steps to our home in the city.

On the second day, my grandfather announced he had to go home. My dad protested but "Papa" was firm. Papa didn't know why, he just knew he had to get back to his blind wife and their adult daughter. My dad reluctantly drove Papa to the bus station in Providence.

The next afternoon I stood on the unfinished porch with my dad watching the rain and wind blow by the house. At five and a half years old, I was holding onto the porch railing and my dad was holding onto me. Suddenly, without making a sound, a tree in the lot across the street toppled over. It didn't snap or crack it just blew over and was uprooted. Then another tree fell silently. My dad had seen enough and immediately took me inside.

Dad gathered me, my mom, and my two older sisters along the inside wall of the dining room, away from the windows, while he stood in the opposite corner by the telephone.

He called the fire department to discuss the large elm next to our house which was leaning precariously. While he was talking, we heard a thump and saw that massive tree fall past the windows. A branch grazed the house but the main part of the tree fell harmlessly into our driveway.

We didn't know it then but we were witnessing the killer hurricane of 1938 that would claim 682 lives from Long Island, Providence and the Southern New England coastline. There was no radar in those days and there had been no public warning of the approaching danger.

For two days, my dad tried in vain to reach Papa but the phone lines were down. Finally, on the third day, dad decided to drive. He told us later he didn't realize how catastrophic this hurricane had been until he approached the ocean.

Where there had once been a row of homes there was now rubble or empty space. The road was obliterated in places by sand and he had to detour around large boats and wharfs left stranded in the middle of the roadway.

He finally arrived in Tiverton only to find that the Old Stone Bridge to the island of Portsmouth was no longer there. He hitched a ride in an open boat.

When he reached the island, he found everything in shambles. Many of the buildings he was familiar with were gone. Dad said he was disoriented. There was so much devastation he wandered around in a state of confusion and apprehension.

Finally, he saw a metal street sign still in place which told him he was at Papa's road. His heart sank, All the cottages on the street were crushed, dislodged or gone.

Then he saw one complete house still standing with minimal damage. It was the one Papa had built himself decades earlier.

Papa said, when he awoke the morning of the storm, he saw the ominous clouds, and boarded up his house, including the cellar windows preventing water from flooding the house and carrying it away. Papa, my grandma and my aunt, rode out the ferocious storm in the dark in that single story house. Some of the shingles were ripped off and the outhouse was gone but that's all.

What had produced that overwhelming urge for my grandfather to return home?

He never tried to explain it. When asked how he knew he had to return home, Papa would just shrug his shoulders and look skyward.

"Something was telling me I had to go home," was all that he would say. He just heeded the message. It is well he did.

Like my Papa, today I pay attention to any strong inner messages. I know the source.

Jody Estes
Providence, RI.

"Whoever listens to me shall dwell safely, and shall be quiet without fear of evil."
 (Proverbs 1:33)

God's Sense of Humor

My Special Reference

I had been working at a shipping company for a couple of years, but because I had studied to be a legal secretary, I was ready to get a job with a law firm. I sought God's guidance to help me find a job where I could utilize my legal training.

During lunch hours, I would take my Bible and head behind the office building where there were benches and fountains. While there, I would often see homeless people and panhandlers.

There was one man in particular who was there every day. Eventually, he came to me and asked what I was reading and I told him. He asked if I was a Jesus freak and I said yes I am. He said I made him feel uncomfortable when he was trying to ask people for money. I told him I had no condemnation for him, but that I thought he seemed able bodied enough to work. I also shared my desire to get a job with a law firm.

We became speaking friends and one day he said, "Since you know God so well, why don't you pray that I get a job." At that moment I put my hand on his shoulder and started praying out loud. "Not here, not now," he protested. I kept praying. That was on a Thursday.

On Monday he came running up to me at lunch. He was clean and groomed and I hardly recognized him. An attorney he had been asking for money had hired him as a custodian.

I was happy for him but I was jealous. I said (silently of course) God, I am the one who wanted a job with a law firm. Have you mixed things up here or what? I thanked God for giving this man a job.

About a week later, the man came to me and said, "I have an interview for you at the law firm. The senior partner needs a secretary."

I thought this would take an act of faith for me to go on an interview he arranged. Were they just humoring him?

Those thoughts vanished immediately because I knew I would do nothing to cause him to waiver in his belief in answered prayers. I was not going to let pride prevent me from going and thereby show a lack of faith. I thanked God for the opportunity, went on the interview, and I was hired on the spot.

The attorneys still tell people that the best employment recommendation they ever had was from a homeless man. I remind them that God alone was my employment agent.

God will answer your prayer when you step out in faith. God also has a wonderful sense of humor.

Carolyn Bourgeois
New Orleans, LA.

"In all your ways acknowledge
God and he will direct your paths."
(Proverbs 3:6)

Lessons from a Red Couch

Dean and I were trying to wait before buying a nice couch set until I got a fulltime job. Our living room consisted of a huge pile of blankets and pillows on the floor. Since I was working from home I had no comfy place to sit all day.

I talked Dean into considering secondhand couches on Craigslist that we could get right away. Our budget was $50. I saw a red couch in great shape online for $75. Dean agreed to go with me to see it.

It had rained that day and the folks selling it had stored it outside under a ripped tarp and it was pretty wet. Dean also noticed a stale smell.

I wanted a couch so badly that I was willing to overlook the smell and the dampness. I thought we could just wash it. Dean was set against it and I was really disappointed. We had a spat.

He said, God has something better in store for us. I told him that I thought he had just missed it and I proceeded to walk off.

Later that night we both apologized and decided to go to Goodwill stores the next day.

The next morning, our cat, Billow, accidently scratched my eyelid (ouch!) We didn't leave until afternoon with me wearing a pirate-like eye patch.

Two Goodwill stores later, no couch. It was near closing time when a sympathetic Goodwill employee told us to check out the Salvation Army store around the corner. Sure enough, there was a red, dry, nice smelling couch on sale for $50. The store was closing in 10 minutes. We agreed this was the couch for us. Everyone at the store was being very nice to me, perhaps because of the eye patch.

We called a friend who came right over in her pickup truck and delivered the couch to our home.

Lessons I learned: be patient, don't grasp so tightly to material things that I blow up at my husband (and look like a fool), and trust God always.

I'm convinced, God actually does care about the little things in my life too.

I look back on all this now and I have a good laugh. I think God is smiling too.

Jessica R. MacLeod
Greensboro, NC.

Road Sign

I recently moved to Minnesota from Florida. As I was driving home from a job interview my mind started to wander.

I thought about my future in this new state. Lord, am I suppose to take this job or the one I interviewed for yesterday? I was getting tired of waiting for what God had for me next. I could feel myself getting anxious thinking about money.

Can I afford to live alone? How much longer can I work part time without health care benefits? How much time off will I get, what about the holidays, and on and on the questions came.

At this point, I realized the beautiful city backdrop of buildings, sparkling in the sunlight, one of my favorite views, somehow, as I looked, my new home city was rushing past my car window. I had relaxed and become lost in my thoughts.

I had missed my exit and was driving in unfamiliar territory.

As I looked around to get my bearings, I saw a bright yellow sign ahead. I struggled to read it, and as I got closer, I thought I saw the word trust.

When I read the billboard, I laughed out loud for there in big letters, and I am not kidding, were the words;

"TRUST ME!" – GOD.

Even though I was traveling seventy miles an hour, I felt like time had just stopped. With a chuckle, I let go of all those doubting thoughts and decided to do what I was told and TRUST HIM.

As I exited the highway and turned my car around to find my way back to familiar surroundings, I knew it was no mistake that I had become distracted and saw that huge billboard.

In that moment of quietness, I recalled that in the morning before the interview, I asked God to reveal himself to me and make it obvious what I was to do.

He made it obvious on a large yellow billboard.

God continues to amaze and amuse me.

Beth Bishop
Minneapolis, MN.

The Avocado

Some folks believe we should never "bother" God with small requests. I discovered otherwise many years ago. Through a strange quirk of events, my wife and I, found ourselves without a refrigerator. We had been given one a few years earlier that worked fine but the original owners returned home and needed one, so we gave it back.

The refrigerator we had for a while was white, our other appliances were all avocado green. I set out to find a refrigerator that matched. I quickly discovered that a new, avocado, side by side was way out of our price range.

After much hapless searching, I collapsed on our couch and prayed, "God, where am I going to find a decent used refrigerator?" Two words flashed across my mind, "Jockey Lot."

The Jockey Lot is a huge flea market about 15 miles from our house. During the many times I had been there, I had never seen large appliances for sale. I questioned this supposed, "God message" and mumbled, "That's crazy. They don't sell stuff like that out there!" Nevertheless, I couldn't let it go. Although the words were clear, I got in my car thinking this trip will likely be a waste of time. However, to be obedient, I drove to Jockey Lot. This massive flea market has little rhyme or reason as to what can be found where. Not wanting to spend hours looking, I headed to the main office. I asked, "Excuse me but do you know of any vendors that sell large appliances out here?"

"Not really." I thanked the clerk and started to leave thinking I heard the wrong message from God when she asked, "What are you looking to buy?"

I replied, "A refrigerator."

"I have a large side by side for sale."

"What color is it," I asked in a state of shock.

"It is avocado green."

Problem solved. Thank you God and forgive me for doubting. You are God and the kind and size of the request to You is irrelevant.Now, whenever I am in the produce section of a grocery store and happen to see a nice green avocado, I stop and smile.

Jim Owens
Anderson, SC.

Tim Struggles with God

Hi, my name is Tim and I'm an alcoholic. On March 22, 2017 I had 24 years of sobriety, an achievement I credit to faithfully participating in Alcoholics Anonymous, and to my higher power, God.

After the death of my amazing wife, some five years ago, I took up walking for exercise. My usual routine is to walk from my house, downtown, across the Ringling Bridge and back. When it is windy or chilly, I take an alternate route, through downtown, around City Island and return home.

My walks, besides exercise, have evolved into a time for meditation and prayer, which has become the most important part of my day. On occasion, I have found myself returning home so absorbed that I have no recollection of the walk itself. These walks are my time with God. It is wonderful.

When walking my alternate route, I pass the marina where there are what I call "rust buckets as well as gorgeous yachts from distant ports. One beautiful Catamaran has printed on stairs leading to the stern, "It's About Time," Newark, Delaware.

One morning, I was meditating over a recurring personal problem. I have an on-going struggle between my ego and God, as to who is going to be in charge of my life each day. I have a choice as to whether I will obey God or my ego. I can, and often do, made the wrong choice. This morning, I was asking God for some help. I'm whispering, "Lord Is my ego blocking me from connecting with you?"

I approached the catamaran as I uttered this question and the transom came in view. What I saw was, "IT'S ABOUT TIM."

The E was not visible until I took another step to read the complete word, TIME. I saw the name of this yacht with a spiritual difference, that gave me the connection with God that I sought. My struggle was over this day, as it always is when I seek Him. My mind was opened by this timely message.

When I let my ego decide. then it is all about TIM.

Tim Lampman
Downtown, Sarasota, Fl.

A Controlled Church Auction

The vestry has asked me to write about the amazing events of Monday, October 31,2016 for inclusion in our church history.

Father John Mears and the congregation at little St. Peter's church in Forestville, New York, left the apostate Episcopal Diocese to join the Anglican Church of North America many years ago.

The Episcopal Diocese continued to claim ownership of this property, which by New York law they were entitled to do. The national Episcopal church leadership approved a rule that would not allow any congregation leaving the Episcopal church to buy the property it occupied.

Jim Fanning, Chancellor of the Diocese, greatly respected Fr. John and was sympathetic to the work being done at St. Peter's. Eventually, (we think with the Chancellor's encouragement) the Diocese decided to put the property up for public auction, giving us a chance to bid. The date was set.

Our vestry and Father White, who had become our pastor after Fr. Mears died, decided to limit the amount we would bid to $15,000 (all the cash we had.)We were told there was a man from Evans coming to bid and someone was flying up from

Florida with plenty of money. His plan was to strip the building of its stained glass windows (valued at $35,000) and remove the ancient timbers and fixtures.

The auction began at 9 A.M. Nearly all the congregation was there. The bidding began and surprisingly there was only one other person bidding against us. The bidding began slowly and when it reached $2700 our Pastor bid $3,000. Suddenly it was quiet. there was no other bid. "Going once, going twice, sold to St. Peter's congregation."

While officials were signing all the legal documents two angry men (including the man from Florida) came in furious they had missed the auction. They mistakenly had gone to the Forestville Clerk's office and not to the Hanover Clerk's office.

You can imagine the cheering and tears from our members because it was God, Who arranged the winning bid for us. God wasn't through blessing our church. Later, after our pastor had shared our story at St. Bartholomew's Church in North Tonawanda, a parishioner came and handed him an envelope containing a check for $3,000. Praise the Lord.

Dorothy Mears, church secretary
Forestville, NY.

A Glass of Wine

A pastor was recalling that he and his wife were dinning out with her best friend from college and her atheist husband who was also a cynic and was always making fun of Christianity.

"The waiter came to the table and asked for our drink order. Three of us asked for ice tea and the skeptic ordered a class of the house wine. After the waiter left, the atheist said mockingly, 'Reverend, too bad Jesus isn't here, he could turn my cheap glass of wine into the best wine.'

"I thought, I'm not going there. I ignored the comment. My wife picked up on the moment and changed the subject. The ladies talked while I sat in silence, while my naysayer smirked.

"Our waiter returned with the beverages and placed three glasses of ice tea on the table in front of us. He turned to the atheist and said, 'I'm sorry sir but we are out of our house wine. My manager apologizes, and said to give you a glass of our very best wine.

True Story
Nashua, NH.
Answer a fool according to his folly, less he be wise in his own mind." (Proverbs 26:5)

Healings

Unshakeable Faith

Shortly after moving my family from the States to Johannesburg, South Africa to work with Bibles For Africa, I woke up with pins and needles and a numbness in my left arm. The feeling was like when people would say, "my arm has fallen asleep." In my case my arm stayed asleep for three weeks and simple tasks were awkward and painful to perform.

I visited the Neurology Department of an academic hospital in Pretoria. I was diagnosed with a pinched nerve in my cervical spine and referred for x-rays. The technician there reminded me that the nominal fee to enter the hospital entitled me to visit as many departments as there was time in that business day at no cost except for pharmaceuticals. I told her I had injured my lumbar spine several years ago. She took x-rays of my lumbar.

The government hospital did not have an MRI machine so I opted to see a radiologist in private practice. The radiologist interpreting the MRI referred me to a local Neurosurgeon, who he highly recommended with the caution, "this guy likes to perform surgeries." My visit to the Neurosurgeon confirmed I had a pinched nerve in the cervical spine but he was stunned when he looked at the lumbar x-rays.

"How do you walk," he asked?
I abruptly answered, "I put one foot in front of the other, the same as you do."

He pointed to the x-ray which showed that the disc between the lowest two vertebrae had disintegrated. He predicted that if I didn't have corrective surgery, I would likely be in a wheelchair in five years.

To treat the cervical spine issue he gave me two options. The first was to admit me to a hospital where I would be heavily sedated while in traction for a week. The second option, which the Neurosurgeon reluctantly mentioned, was a home traction kit which I could use over time.
As I drove home, I simply said, "Father' I cannot subject myself to whatever is involved with a weeklong sedation. As for the home traction kit at home, I have a three-year old and a one-year-old. I would become a human gym set. This won't work either. I'm simply going to trust You God."From that day on the pins and needles went away.

This happened 22 years ago. Today, I'm back living in America and working without limitation or hindrance. Through the grace of God, I continue to put one foot in front of the other.

Mark Walker
Antwerp, OH.

Fear or Faith

It had been 16 years since I visited any gynecologist. I had no problems up until last year, when I began having irregular bleeding and heavy periods. I had several tests and they found that I had fibroids and a cyst on my ovary.

My doctor suggested in November that I have a full hysterectomy. This would be my fifth surgery on my abdomen so I would have to sign a paper indicating that I understood that there would be more risk involved. I asked about keeping my ovaries so that I wouldn't go into full menopause.

My doctor said given my age and the size of the cyst (that may require surgery to be removed in the future), she recommended taking everything.

I struggled with this decision until the day before my scheduled surgery, January 30. I had asked the Lord over and over again if I was doing the right thing. To be honest with you, I was afraid. It was also a pride issue. I didn't want anyone to know, because it would look as though I was weak or defeated. I chose not to tell anyone but my family.

I had these thoughts, that were not of God, telling me that things would not go right and I would die on the operating table. I was upset and I laid awake at night worrying.

I picked up the Bible looking for an answer. I went to several church services seeking solace but the negative thoughts became worse than ever. It was like the more positive encouragement I received the more negative I became. This whole thing was overwhelming.
My pastor always says that the battle is in the mind. Let me tell you, a war was going on in my head.

I decided to go to a women's group, and afterwards I would call the doctor to tell her I decided to delay the surgery.

At the women's group, Sandy who has always been such a comfort to me and my family, came up to me and said she was happy to see me there, and asked me if I would now be able to come on Tuesdays.

I told her what was going on, and when she began to talk I knew the Lord was speaking to me through her because a peace and comfort came over me. The negative attacks immediately stopped. She prayed for me and I was relaxed and knew what I had to do, and it was right. I would have the operation.

My surgery went extremely well, and I was up walking in eight hours. I had such comfort knowing that Jesus was with me.

The nurses commented on how fast I was up and walking. I knew it was the Lord giving me the ability to get around so quickly. I went home two days later.

When I returned a week later to have the staples removed, my doctor shared what she didn't want to tell me on the telephone. She said, they tested everything that was taken out and discovered I had cancerous cells in the my uterus.

This is an extremely fast growing cancer. Every time the uterus sheds, the cancer grows and starts spreading into the blood. The recommended procedure for this is a full hysterectomy. What they found was that the cancerous cells were still intact and concentrated in one area of the uterus.

My doctor told me that I was lucky that someone was watching over me. I said I know God is. She kept saying you are cured over and over. We cried and held one another.

My doctor had no idea that the cancer cells were there. I asked her why it wasn't seen on all the tests. She said it was located where no test would have detected it. I cried more. If I had not had this operation, I would be looking at 5-6 months.

If my doctor had not taken my ovaries she would have had to go back in and get them. When cancer is present, the best operation is actually cutting your abdomen (what I had) because when they do the other surgery there is a risk of dropping cells.

What an awesome God we have. Not only did He heal me of something that would have killed me but He didn't even let me know that I had it. My family never had to go through that worry and anguish.

I do not have to know everything. I just have to trust Him. All the glory to God because He knew and no one else did.

I am so grateful that words can't describe it.

Jackie Harmon
Richmond, VA.

Image Bearer

It was October 2. It was my day off and it was my birthday. I was also a month and a half into therapy for burnout and depression.

I love to garden and there was a particular flower bed that irritated me. I was determined this day to weed, plant and mulch that piece of the garden.

While on my knees pulling weeds, God brought to mind a story about a mom picking up her daughter from work. The daughter was on her knees stocking a shelf. Two men walked by the end of the aisle and she heard one man say to the other, "That's where a woman should be, down on her knees."

The words and the imagery pierced my heart. It was my story. I had been told who I was based on someone's definition of what I could and could not do. The tears came and with every weed I yanked I became more determined to remove the lies from my heart about who I was. I cried out to God.

Most of my negative messages had come through religious, male authoritative figures in my life. Still on my knees by that garden, I looked up to the sky and asked, " How can I be created in your image when you are, when you are...ALL MALE."

I stiffened, looked around, but lightning didn't strike, so I continued weeding not expecting an answer.

What came to mind was a picture of Jesus on His knees washing the dirty feet of his disciples. My tears began to flow only this time they were not tears of anguish but tears of healing and pure joy.

I felt as if the very hand of God had touched my heart and healed it.

At that moment, I realized that Jesus, though male, understood me more than anyone. He, the King of kings, went down on His knees and took the lowly position of a servant to wash dirty feet. He most certainly understood me. He made me and knew every intimate detail about me from the beginning.

That day, Jesus healed me. He restored my rightful position as a worthy child of God to come alongside as co-image bearers. He had a purpose and a plan for my life, and it was not based on what others said I could do, but based on who God said I was through Christ.

Janae Shatley Camp
Paragould, AR.
Taken from *Image Wearers to Image Bearers*
Reprinted with Permission.

Ruben's Miracle Healings

My Dad, Ruben Beachy, bent over to get into his bed when the most excruciating pain imaginable hit him. He felt like he was being crushed from every side and it became hard to breathe.

He was rushed to the hospital. The diagnosis was he had suffered a Type B aortic dissection where the lining within the aorta tears and creates a false lumen where blood flows between the layers of lining instead of inside the artery, preventing blood from reaching limbs and vital organs.

Reuben's dissection was extensive. The tear started from the mid arch and went down the aorta to the lower abdomen and into the kidney. His situation was critical. He was taken by ambulance to Tampa General and was taken into surgery.

We sent out prayer requests to family and friends who interceded for Reuben for the five hours he was in surgery. Praise the Lord, he made it through. Little did we know, the hard part was beginning.

The next 48 hours would be the longest hours of our lives. The surgeon explained a lumbar drain was inserted to drain fluid off the spine. We were told Reuben needed to be laying flat on his back and if he moved while the drain was not clamped he would become paralyzed.

Four of us took shifts in the ICU 24 hours a day over two days keeping him calm and explaining over and over why he had to remain still.

After those stressful days, the lumbar drain was removed, the pain meds were weaned and we started seeing progress. Reuben was discharged a week later to recover at home.

However, early Saturday morning, November 28th, Reuben woke up with severe chest pains. We called 911 and he was rushed to Sarasota Memorial Hospital. He was diagnosed with a Type A aortic dissection which started at the beginning of the endograft from the previous surgery and tore the other way to the heart. Type A is often fatal.

SMH stabilized his blood pressure and put him on a helicopter to Tampa General for immediate surgery. His heart stopped in flight. CPR was performed and his heart started beating again.

Upon arriving at Tampa General he was taken to the emergency room to stabilize him for the Operating Room. However, over the next fifty minutes, he coded (heart stopped) three more times. At this point the doctors were not hopeful he would survive long enough to get to the operating room.

As a last ditch effort to stabilize him, the doctors decided to attempt to aspirate the blood from the sac around the heart by performing a procedure called a Pericardialcentesis. A needle is inserted through the chest and into the sac and the blood is drawn out with a syringe. The survival rate is very rare.

Following the miracle of a successful Pericardialcentesis Reuben was taken into the OR and placed on a heart lung machine. From noon to four we waited and prayed. We knew that whatever happened, God is good, but oh how we were interceding for God to spare his life,

At 4:00 the surgeon told us Reuben had survived but we wouldn't know until tomorrow, once he was no longer sedated or on a ventilator, if there had been any brain damage suffered from the four times his heart had stopped.

When we arrived at the hospital the next morning at seven, we were shocked to see Reuben off the ventilator, no longer sedated, talking and even making jokes.

This healing has been one miracle after another; the fact that he survived his heart stopping in the helicopter, and three more times in the emergency room, then the pericardialcentesis, surviving the heart lung machine, the reconstruction of his entire aorta and all the blood vessels going to his brain and then coming out of all this with no brain damage. All these miracles have doctors from around the hospital following the case from beginning to end because it continues to defy all expectations.

Oh the power of God and the power of prayer. Based on the information from friends, family, pastors, prayer teams at various church congregations we estimate more than 18,000 people we interceding for Reuben. On December 7, 2015 Reuben came home from the hospital.
God answered all our prayers and we are rejoicing for the time we will continue to have with Reuben.

Melissa Beachy
Washington, DC and Southwest, Fl.

"Whatever things you ask in prayer, believing, you will receive." (Matthew 21:22)

Grandfather's Healing

I was living in St. Paul, Minnesota when I received a call from my mother that my grandfather was very sick. He had four blood clots and cancer and was given two days to live.

I poured some healing oil on a handkerchief and prayed over it with my friend Rodney. I sent it over night by Fed Ex to my mother at the hospital in Colorado Springs. I included a note to my mother instructing her to place the handkerchief under grandfather's pillow and to pray over him.

When she visited her dad's hospital room she went me one better. She folded the handkerchief carefully and placed it on his forehead. She prayed, "In the name of Jesus, be Healed." She prayed emphatically "IN THE NAME OF JESUS, BE HEALED!"

The next day, my older sister Katie walked into our grandfather's room. He greeted her waving the handkerchief, "Look what Dan did," he said. The cancer and the blood clots were gone. It wasn't me, it was God. My grandfather lived several more years before he was called home. Praise the Lord.

Dr. Daniel Van Ingen
Colorado Springs, CO.

Trusting God

A Moment Of Faith

In 1946, I was stationed in the Aleutian Islands as a chaplain for the United States Air Force. Our particular island , Shemya, was shaped like an oyster and was just large enough to have one important airstrip.

One night, a tremendous earthquake broke open the deep water of the Bay of Alaska and sent tons of surge water (a tsunami) toward our island. The high flood water, much higher than our island, was to hit us at about 3 a.m.

We had 3,600 men on the island, but only one surface craft for about 200. The idea of evacuation was abandoned.

Hundreds of men and officers gathered in the chapel on the high side of the island. Our highest elevation was about 18 feet and we were warned to expect a wave of about 40 feet.

Every light was on in the chapel.

We had both large and small prayer services and the men periodically sang songs of all faiths and wrote letters. Many men sat alone thinking of their families and what the impending death by drowning would be like.

At about 4 a.m. the wave came. There was a strong gush of wind and high water, but nothing like the predicted 40 feet. The island of Adak, lying 400 miles to our east broke the wave in two, with one half going into the Bearing Sea and the other toward Hawaii.

We were spared. Lots of water (ranging from15 to 18 feet) and a lot of mopping up, but there were no casualties. Not a single life was lost.

The water came as far as the Chapel steps and no further.

Our faith had been lifted by total trust and dependence on God, and the Lord came to our rescue.

Lionel W. Nelson, USAF retired
Shema Island, AK.

More than a Golf Story

Brad's celebrity golf status is that he was the first golfer to lose a national title to Tiger Woods.

The year was 1991, and Brad Zwetschke was ranked number two behind Tiger in the U.S. Junior Amateur golf. In the championship match Brad was three up after five holes, and two up at the turn at Bay Hill in Orlando. It would be the first of many well publicized comebacks for Tiger, who tied the match and defeated Brad on the first playoff hole.

"Coming out of school all I wanted to do was play golf and party. I lived the wild life," Brad recalled.

Along the way he met Christina Mauldin, a preacher's daughter from the South side of Chicago. Brad is also from Chicago. Within a year and a half they were married.

"She thought she was marrying a golf professional and I thought I was marrying an entertainer from Black Television." (Christina had done a stint on the program Heart & Soul.)

" My wife is a strong Christian and my most loyal supporter. She accompanied me on tour, which is arduous, lots of travel and expensive. Sometimes we slept in our van because we couldn't afford hotels.

"In November, 2001, we were touring in Australia and we went into a little church in Brisbane. The preacher's message was based on John 21. The message spoke to me, especially when

Jesus asks Peter, 'Do you love me as much as these' (referring to the fish Peter and his friends had just caught?) I identified with Peter who was being asked to give up fishing. I felt I was being asked to put down my golf clubs.

"Three months later I was driving to the Canadian Tour Qualifying Tournament when I heard a message on the radio quoting John 21. Again I felt the message was speaking to me.

"I played in the tournament but I did not qualify. My heart wasn't in the game anymore. I quit golf.

"With the encouragement of my father-in law, I enrolled in New Orleans Theological Seminary. He too had been called to the ministry by John 21."

In August, 2005, four months before Brad was to graduate, Hurricane Katrina devastated New Orleans. With two children and Christina eight months pregnant, Brad borrowed a neighbor's van and fled the powerful storm. He drove to Beatrice, Alabama where a pastor friend took them in.

"We lost everything in the hurricane, as our apartment was completely flooded. But God spared our family.

"Then another kind of flood hit. I could not stop the flow of gifts of clothing, food and furniture that poured in on us.

"When it was time for Christina to have our fourth child we moved to Bradenton , Florida to be close to the doctor who had delivered our other children.

"I took a job as student intern in evangelism and finished my final year with the seminary on line.

In December, 2006, my classmates and I returned to New Orleans and received our degrees. Later, I became the voluntary chaplain to the Cincinnati Reds farm team that was in Sarasota, Florida.

"God has used everything in my life for His purposes. Golf had been my idol. Now I'm pictured in golf magazines holding a Bible. It took a while for me to accept God's forgiveness and his grace. That has been huge growth for me.

"Tiger became the king of golf. My notoriety as being the first to lose a national title to Tiger still brings invitations to speak at golf dinners and men's retreats where I get to tell people about the King of kings."

Brad Zwetschke
Kansas City, KS.
(Brad is now a U.S. Army Chaplain)

"Simon do you love Me more than these?"
"Yes Lord, You know that I love You."
Jesus said," Feed My lambs." (John 21:15)

Will Howard's Story

I was born in 1947 in Easton, Maryland, a few doors down from the boarding house where my folks first met nine years earlier. Growing up here everyone knew your name.

When I went to the University of Maryland, the Associated Press (AP) hired me as a campus stringer. My most memorable story was when the Students for a Demographic Society announced in the campus newspaper, The Diamond Back, that they would occupy the Skinner building on Thursday at 10 a.m. The AP said stay on that story it could be big.

The kids came in dressed like everybody else. At 3 p.m.,The University cancelled all classes in the Skinner Building and ordered all university personnel to leave the building. A professor let me use his second story office and phone.

At dusk, Maryland State Troopers arrived and completely encircled the building. An officer read the Maryland Trespass Act, and announced that anyone who did not leave in the next 15 minutes would be arrested and put in jail until the next day for a hearing. That meant me.

I scampered down the stairs and told an SDS person I'm going to cover this from outside They laughed because they had barricaded all the doors. After I ran upstairs to call AP, the doors exploded and the state police entered. I stayed on the phone with AP when the office door opened and two state troopers came in. I said "I'm with the Associated Press. Here talk to my boss he is on the phone." The Trooper took the telephone and hung it up.

I was the last one out with a state trooper on each arm. I was lead down the steps past the glaring lights of the TV cameras. My mother was sure to be watching. I noticed that the head trooper was a friend of my Mom's. It was Lt. Colonel Paul Randall. I said, "Hi Colonel Randall." He turned around and said, "William, Your dad told me you were here working for the Associated Press. Is that what you are doing?""Yes Sir."

He said to the troopers, " I'll take this prisoner."

He took me back into the Skinner Building. While he was looking around at the damage I asked, "Am I under arrest?"

He said, "No, you are a member of the press."

The next day, The Baltimore News American carried my story on the front page and the AP gave me a byline. I wasted no time calling the City

Editor, telling him who I was and that I was interested in a part time job and would work fulltime in the summer. He said, "Be here at 9a.m."

I was hired and assigned to cover three police districts in the city. The Western district was the worse. It was the number one murder capital of the United States. I covered a lot of exciting stories, including one time being in the back seat of a detective's car, chasing bank robbery suspects at ninety miles an hour with guns drawn. .

One day, on my way home, nature called. The closest public rest room I knew about was in a parking garage. I walked into the men's room, brightly lit and walked straight over to a urinal. As I did, I realized there was fresh cigarette smoke in the air. Three stall doors opened at once and out came three men. I had the same walkie-talkie that police carry. I grabbed and slapped it on that urinal. It worked, all three left. I was so scared it would take hours before I was able to accomplish my original purpose for going into that room.

Weeks later, I was promoted to downtown writer. This was special, as I was given a column called, Man About Town. Before I could write my first column, I received a phone call from my father who said to come home, there was a family emergency. When family calls, you "gotta go." I received a one year leave of absence from the newspaper. I took an apartment on Dover Street back in Easton.

In the mid-80's I spent a lot of time across the street in a restaurant where I met Jerome Nicolosi, the new manager of the Tidewater Inn, who made no secret that he was a born again Christian. One day at lunch he asked, "If you died tomorrow where would you go?"

I said, "The Lord welcomes to Heaven those people who do more good than bad and I think I've done more good than bad so I guess I would go to Heaven."

He said, "That is not what it says in the Bible."

I said, "Really?"He read to me, John 3: 3; "Truly, I say to you, unless one is born again he will not see the Kingdom of Heaven."

I knew I was not born again. He suggested I have a personal relationship with Jesus Christ. How do you do that? I would send up lots of prayers but I wasn't hearing much coming back. Jerome said, "Invite Him into your heart."
I struggled with that. I had been in church for more than 20 years and was an Elder of my church. We did very little Bible study, so I had to research this. I did, and I found out he was right. So one night

while I was in bed (next to my wife Dorothy) I invited Jesus Christ into my life.

It wasn't until two weeks later that I realized what I had done. I was joking with a friend. I used salty words. As soon as those words came out of my mouth I was convicted. There was a voice in my head that said, "THAT IS NOT HOW CHRISTIANS TALK."I said, startled, "WHAT?" I heard again; "THAT IS NOT HOW CHRISTIANS TALK."

I was immediately embarrassed and apologized to my friend who was very puzzled.

That voice inside me, I would learn after reading the Bible, was the Holy Spirit, Who would guide me to a Bible preaching church. He would guide me to a lot of things.

I prayed and asked God to guide me to a new career. I wanted to be more creative, and travel with my wife. I had no idea what I was asking, but God would answer my prayer in a couple of years. I came up with the idea of shooting a video about Talbot County and putting it in hotel rooms. By the end of that year it was very successful. This new business in 1992 led me to become acquainted with a gentleman named Ron Ensminger.

He was the cofounder and president of Sat
(Satellite) Seven and had moved the national
headquarters to Easton. Sat Seven is a Christian
Broadcasting Company airing programs in Farsi and
Arabic to the Middle East.

He suggested I shoot a video for tourists and come
to the Middle East and explore this. Dorothy and I,
and our son James, who was 15, flew to Beirut,
Lebanon. We were picked up at the airport by
officials from Sat Seven. We were taken on a tour
of the city and at a stoplight I noticed a building
riddled with bullet holes. I instinctively grabbed my
camera and my guide said, "Freeze! Don't move a
muscle!" I was startled. He told me to release my
camera and sit back in my seat. I did. Then I saw a
sentry with a machine gun looking right at me.

My guide said, "What you saw on your right was
Hezbollah HQ and that sentry would have arrested
you and taken you to jail and you would have been
deported."

In Cairo the rules were different. We were picked
up at our hotel and a bodyguard with a machine gun
sat in the front seat. We went to Sharm El Sheik and
stayed in an Italian resort.

They were setting up a buffet in this restaurant
when I took out my camera and tripod and started

taking several shots. The general manager came over, and I told him I was shooting a tourism video to be shown in the United States. After that we were friends. His name was Muhammad. That night, I introduced Muhammad to Ron as the president of Sat Seven. Muhammad's face turned serious. He said, "I have a wife and family and I do not let them watch Sat Seven." He railed for twenty minutes on the importance of the Muslim Religion before leaving. What he said I found chilling.

That night I was awakened by that inner voice and told to deliver a Bible to Muhammad. I had purchased a Bible in Beirut at the International Bible Association. It was a New Testament in paperback. I told my wife what my intentions were and she bolted out of bed and said, "You are going to get us all arrested and put in an Egyptian jail." I said," I've got direct orders to do this."

The next morning, while strolling with Ron, I explained what I was about to do. Ron said, "Are you sure about this?"
I said, "Every molecule in my body wants to deliver this Bible to Muhammad."He said, "You could be putting our company in danger. We might lose our license to broadcast. Do it this way. Tell him it is between you two, don't even mention Sat Seven."

I asked for Muhammad. He came over and I said, "I've had a good time here. I have a gift for you." Muhammad said, "You have a gift for me?"

"I know you have your book and I have my book but I want this to be a gift to you, from me to you, nothing to do with him," I said, pointing to Ron.

I gave him the Bible. He turned around and stared at it very intentionally. He looked at me and said, "I have been praying for six months for someone to bring me a Bible." He embraced me with a big hug. Muhammad asked Ron when he would be back. Ron said probably in a year. Muhammad said, "I will be a Christian when you return."

This tells me three things:

1.My God hears everyone's prayers.
2. I have a relationship with Jesus Christ and I know when I die I will go to Heaven.
3.God protected me my entire life to deliver that Bible to Mohammad and this message to you.

Will Howard
Easton, MD.
Excerpts from his talk at the Mayor's Prayer Breakfast, 2010.

Debbie Hears from God

I love my God. He is my everything. So when people would share how God clearly spoke to them, I would be puzzled and wonder, "Why isn't God speaking to me?"

In the fall of 2005, a thought came to mind, should I consider returning to St. Louis (I had been in Florida for five years.) I had left St. Louis after experiencing a painful divorce and a lot of heartache. I didn't feel it was a place I would ever return to live.

 Let me tell you, it is awesome what you can hear from God when you are quiet and consistently seeking his Word.

I was clearly hearing from God that he wanted me to return permanently. I had not experienced this before, so I wanted to make sure I was getting it right. I decided to go to St. Louis for Christmas.

On my trip, I asked God to reveal to me through my friend Mary that this is what he wanted me to do. Mary truly walks and talks with God. Over the past five years she never asked me, "when are you coming home?"

After a lunch with five lady friends, Mary pulled me aside and said, "Debbie, God has put you on my heart. It is time you came home."

Trembling, I said, "One problem, I need a job." Mary told me that two days earlier, a nurse recruiter friend, who she hadn't seen in months, showed up at her front door. She would always call ahead. She told Mary she didn't know why she was there but had a strong urge to visit. During the conversation, she revealed she was in need of a Nurse Case Manager and did Mary know of anyone. Mary told her she was having lunch with me in two days and she would bring it up. Mary said , "Fax your resume to Karen (the recruiter) and let God do the rest."

I told Mary what I had been praying for and how she revealed God's desire for me. We both began to cry tears of joy and praised God for his goodness.

I returned to Florida, listed my condo for sale, had a telephone interview and was hired for the Nurse Case Manager position. I moved to St. Louis.

Spend time with the Lord. Pray, read scripture, and then, most importantly, be still, and listen. We MUST be obedient to God's will in our life.

Debbie Houston
St. Louis, M0.

Christine's Laments

The surgeon delivered the news no woman wants to hear, " you have Invasive Carcinoma, Mammary Type with Lobular Features."

This was totally unexpected, My family and I were to begin an unchartered journey. The first week, I was busy with medical appointments, tests and beginning treatment. Toxic chemicals were pumped into my body to destroy the cancer cells.

I went to work as usual (as a school administrator) and John, my husband, and I continued to care for our family of eight children, ranging in ages from 22 to two).

God, as always, met our needs in so many ways , especially through the love and support of family and many friends.

In the book of Psalms, David laments over his troubles. David uses such words as vindicate, rejected, downcast and disturbed. There is nothing in Psalm 43 to indicate that God changed anything at all for David.

Yet David comes to the conclusion, "Put your hope in God for I will yet praise Him, my Savior and my God."

I have learned that God can handle our lament. I think it is important for people of faith to express their lament to God. I am not certain why, but it has proven to be an important part of my journey of faith.

Prayer, I use to think, was answered if God fixed it, settled it, repaired it, paid it, or healed it the way I imagined it should be.
I've learned God doesn't do things my way but God does promise to be with me always and to provide me with what I need and when I need it.

Did I ever say, "Why me God? Why do I have cancer?" Well not exactly. I've seen too many faithful brothers and sisters face their own challenges and find grace and strength to survive.

What has lamenting looked like for me? It sounds like this:

One more thing breaks down unexpectedly: "I wish I didn't have to deal with this. I don't have the energy."

We face one more parenting challenge. "Really Lord why can't this go more smoothly right now."

A pot of spaghetti sauce falls out of the fridge on my 50th birthday. "Why God?
Yet will I praise Him."

I drop mascara making a mess of my outfit for church. I sit down and sob and sob.

And yes, I have sent messages to friends saying, "I wish this was not happening."

I believe God can handle it all. The sweetness of my journey is seeing what God has done in and through me because of every twist and turn in this life that has caused me to lament.

This hasn't always been easy, but God keeps meeting my every need.

I have lamented, I do lament. I will probably lament again. I believe the richness in my relationship with Christ has come primarily through the repeated practice of lamenting, and then declaring;

"FOR I WILL YET PRAISE HIM."

Christine Bradford
Buffalo, NY.

"Why my soul, are you downcast?
Why so disquieted within me
Put your hope in God,
for I will yet praise him, who is the
health of my countenance and my
God."
(Psalm 43:5)

Jack Livingston's Journey

In 1972, I was hitchhiking across our beautiful country. A truck driver, who picked me up, picked up another fellow who talked me into coming along with him to Jackson Hole, Wyoming. This is an amazing place near Yellowstone National Park.

We were both Hippies, interested in getting high and enjoying life. If you were a youth in Jackson Hole, you were either a "Roper" or a "Doper." I spent a wonderful year in this special spot.

One night, I thought I heard a far away radio station promoting a Pink Floyd concert to take place in Sidney, Montana. I set off alone to hitchhike there. Turned out there was no concert.

Leaving Sidney, I set out to tour the Black Hills of South Dakota. I received a ride from a trucker to a little town called Belle Fourche. He left me off at dusk with no chance for another ride till dawn.

I went to a diner for a bowl of chili, and after that to the gas station next door which was open all night. On duty was Steve, a young fellow, who engaged me in conversation. He let me rest in the bunk room in the back they had for tired truckers.

In the morning, he drove me to Rock Springs for breakfast and then to his parents home where he lived with about six other siblings.

I stayed with them that weekend, hanging out with my new friend, going with him to work at the gas station, eating with the family when Steve was there. I even went to church with them on Sunday.

Boy did I have an opportunity to see Christians up close, to hear the sincerity in Steve's father's prayers at table and his mom's practical compassion toward me. They all were so accepting of me, surprisingly so.

I heard the Gospel presented in a manner that wasn't rushed. We discussed, we debated, we shared. The Jesus I learned about from Steve and his family was a humble servant yet the Sovereign of the Universe.

I took a step of accepting the Lord into my heart by saying a prayer. I think of that moment as my, "mustard seed of faith."

I didn't claim to believe in Jesus, I no longer disbelieved. I thought, 'If Jesus is the Living God and all powerful, I'd be a fool to turn my back on Him.' I reasoned, "I'll say this prayer of acceptance and see what happens."

Afterwards, I didn't give up my freewheeling lifestyle or call myself a Christian. Amazingly however, when I let Jesus "into my heart," in that little prayer, don't you know that the Holy Spirit actually did come.

How do I know that the Holy Spirit came into me?

Major changes started happening. For instance, I had been subject to seizures resulting from a brain operation I had a year before. Now, I would experience a warning aura and then either the feeling would pass or the seizure would come. This was frightening for me.

When the warning aura came I found myself calling to Jesus for help from a place deep within. That had never happened to me before.

I was hooked on cigarettes and could never quit for very long. But this time I switched to pipe smoking and eventually was able to stop smoking altogether.

I became curious enough about Jesus to buy a New Testament and I started reading, this time with faith that what I was reading was true.

Two years later, I found myself in San Anselmo, California.

For a month I had been going to home groups, listening to Derek Prince, reading C.S. Lewis', "Mere Christianity" and the "Book of Daniel."

One Wednesday at home group, I was strongly urged to accept the Lord.

"He's calling you, and He is not obligated to call again," the group leader cautioned.

I considered responding but did not act.

That Friday, July 11, 1975, I was wandering alone on a seminary campus near where I was staying when I had the experience of hearing God's voice in my inner being.

I heard: "I HAVE ALWAYS LOVED YOU, AND YOU HAVE NEVER LOVED ME."

The words kind of broke me, even though I felt it was logically impossible for me to love God without His help.

But now that help was being provided though Jesus. who was present with me and guiding me through this "audience" with the Father.

I resolved to love and follow Jesus and to love God.

Two days later, in church, I formalized my decision.

The caution of the care group leader that the Lord was not obligated to repeat His call was appropriate, by the way.

I believe that had I failed to take his words seriously, I might likely have begun drifting away from Jesus.

Jack Livingston

Jackson, WY, Rock Springs, SD, San Anselmo, CA.

It Is a Small World

The first time we ministered to Audrey was at the Florida Correctional facility in Lowell, Florida. Audrey was one of many women for whom we provided spiritual guidance and encouragement through message and song. At one of our services, she made a recommitment to God. She began taking our correspondence Bible study.

Audrey completed her sentence and was released from prison. It was two years after her release, around the time we were getting ready to have our annual banquet, that she wrote me a letter thanking us for our ministry to her in prison. I responded and invited her to speak at the banquet.

While at the banquet, Audrey informed us she had relatives in Tampa and was hoping to put in a transfer and relocate from her present job to Tampa. We all offered prayers for her transfer.

Later, Audrey called us and told us that they offered her a position in Sarasota and she wanted to know what I thought about it. I told her to take it as a stepping stone to Tampa. She accepted the position. We got Audrey involved with our church and offered counsel and assistance whenever we could. She found a room for rent and began her new job.

At this point, Audrey did not have a car so she used either a bus or a cab to get to and from work. However, whenever Mitch, my assistant, and I would go out of town, we would leave the ministry car Mitch drove with her, and we would pick it up upon our return.

One time, when Mitch went to get the car, he found Audrey sleeping in the back seat. After talking with her, he discovered that her landlady had been locking her out periodically and Audrey was afraid to say anything for fear of causing trouble, so, she just slept in the car.

I talked with my wife, Jill, and we decided we would help Audrey get her own place. We invited her to live in our home until she raised enough money to afford her own apartment.

Making a decision to bring Audrey into our home was a big step of faith and obedience for Jill and me. We had done this with someone else and it hadn't work out. In fact we agreed never again. But, "never say never" when you're controlled by a merciful God. All we knew is that Audrey needed help and we had the resources.

We gave as Christ has given to us. Consequently, we continued seeking God for a sign that we did the right thing.

After getting to know Audrey better, we learned she had been married to a professional football player for 17 years. They had two sons. During a very difficult divorce her sons, age 16 and 13, both committed suicide.

When we had met Audrey, she was recovering from the loss of her sons and finishing a 14-month prison term instigated by her husband. who charged her with "grand theft " of their own car.

One day, while I was on a road trip, Jill called to say Audrey's mother died in Tampa and that Audrey was going to join her father and the rest of the other family at the funeral. Audrey's father and mother were divorced. When I returned home, Audrey told me that her father met me in Washington, DC.

It dawned on me that my last visit to D.C. was in October of 1997 at the Promise Keeper Stand-in-the-Gap rally. Surely, in the midst of more than a million men, I could not have met her father.

I recalled an occasion when one speaker asked us men to turn to someone nearby and pray for reconciliation among ethnic groups. Consequently, Mitch and I turned to two gentlemen (one Caucasian and one Black) in back of us and began praying. We prayed for everything from ethnic reconciliation to family protection and good health.

I hadn't thought much of that moment except that I felt the power of God strongly in our prayers. The Caucasian gentlemen asked if he could take a picture to remember this time. I said, "sure, as long as you will mail me one."

I recently received that picture and it was still in the envelope on my desk. I brought the picture to. She pointed to the black gentleman and shouted, "That's my dad! That's my dad!"

With moist eyes we knew that "It's a small world after all." For Jill and me, this moments was our confirmation that Audrey was suppose to be in our home. For Audrey, her faith was increased for she knew God was working in her life.

God miraculously demonstrated His love for Audrey. He will do the same for each of us. I pray that this testimony will encourage you.

Whatever you are going through, remember God loves you and cares for you, and He is in control. God will always work evil for our good, and good for our better. Put your hope and trust in Jesus. He will never fail you.

Rev. Art Hallett
Hallett Prison Ministries

"God Can Use Us"

Ashley Smith, widowed at age 26, had more than her share of troubles, bad choices and tragedies.

Her grandparents raised her while her mother had troubles of her own. Ashley was raised in the church and attended frequently. As a teenager she began acting out and hanging with the wrong crowd. She was arrested for theft and driving under the influence.

She attended college in Georgia but left after a few months to marry Mack Smith, a carpenter. The couple settled in Augusta and had a daughter, Paige. Her husband hung with a tough crowd and in 2001 he was stabbed and died in Ashley's arms.

She moved in with her mother, leaving Paige with an aunt to provide a more stable upbringing for her daughter. More troubles followed and Ashley moved out.

Her life began improving. She completed a six-month medical assistant training course, was working two jobs in Duluth, had her own apartment, and was visiting her daughter regularly.

In the wee hours of Saturday, March 12, 2005, her

world stopped. She was returning to her apartment when a man with a gun appeared out of the darkness. Her first reaction was to scream but her assailant silenced her and told her, "be quiet and I won't hurt you."

Ashley didn't know it then but the man was Brian Nichols, a murder suspect who the day before shot up a Fulton County courtroom, killing a judge, two others and later a federal agent.
Nichols bound Ashley and placed her in the bathtub, which is what he had allegedly done with another woman before he killed her.

Ashley pleaded for her life so her daughter wouldn't become an orphan. She told him, "my husband died four years ago and if you hurt me my little girl won't have a mommy or a daddy."

Nichols, released her from the tub, asking her questions and for the next several hours the two sat in the kitchen talking about the killings, families and God. They watched news reports.

"I can't believe that is me on there," Nichols commented, looking at the TV, "I'm already a dead man."

Ashley related how her faith helped her through her life's challenges. She told him about a book she was reading, *The Purpose Driven Life,* a best seller written by Pastor Rick Warren.

She opened to chapter 33, and read aloud:

"We serve God by serving others."

Nichols asked her to read that sentenced again. She did and continued to read from the chapter about how real servants act. Nichols listened, occasionally raising a question or asking her to repeat something she had just read.

How must Ashley have felt when she read silently these poignant words in that chapter:

"When God puts someone in need right in front of you, he is giving you the opportunity to grow in servant hood. Great opportunities to serve never last long. They pass quickly, sometimes never to return again. You may only get one chance to serve that person, so take advantage of the moment."

That is exactly what Ashley set out to do.

She made a batch of pancakes and the two of them discussed many of the points in the book.

She told him, "You are in my apartment for a reason. God can use you to spread His word to others. It is a miracle you are here and you can fill your own Godly purpose by going to prison and sharing the Word of God with other inmates who need to hear it."

She also pleaded with him to let her visit her daughter who would worry if she missed her morning visit Incredulously, Nichols permitted Ashley to leave her apartment so she could see her daughter. Once outside, she called 911 and the police apprehended her captor who surrendered without a struggle.

This amazing true experience captivated the attention of the national and international media. It touches us for it is a real life example of reason trumpeting madness, hope replacing hopelessness, peace prevailing over violence.

Two weeks later Ashley was honored at the Georgia Capitol by elected officials, and law enforcement officers, for her courage. She was humble in accepting praise and the reward check for leading to Nichols arrest. She said, "First, I want to thank my Lord and Savior, Jesus Christ for His love and grace. My life is a testament that God can use us even in the midst of tragedy and miracles happen."

Duluth, GA.
(Compiled from media reports.)

A Life Change for a Young Girl

Growing up, my parents did not go to church, but my Aunt Shirley did and she would send someone to pick me up whenever she could.

The summer I was ten years old, my grandfather surprised me with the gift of a week at church camp. I had never been outside of New Castle, so this was a huge deal.

I remember being on the bus to the Slippery Rock camp and being very happy. There was another young girl who was not very happy and she kept giving me mean looks. I started giving her mean looks too. I didn't feel happy any longer. I felt angry at this little girl.

On the way to camp, the bus stopped at a church. I asked why and was told some people were going to be baptized because they believed in Jesus and wanted to live in heaven with him. I said I wanted to accept Jesus and go to heaven too. Something came over me after I was baptized.

When I came out of the church, I spotted the girl I was mad at and I didn't feel angry any more. I smiled at her and she smiled back. The bad feelings were all gone. I felt different. My heart was full.

That week at camp we had to work and earn points for our team by learning Bible verses and doing our chores. I remember how happy I felt and how I wanted to help everybody learn their verses and earn points, no matter what team they were on.

I felt so much love, I didn't want the camp to end. At the end of
the week I was chosen as the best girl camper.

I clearly had a transition in my life that summer.

When I was in my twenties, I was in Sunday school and I read a sign on the wall.

The sign said, "He is alive."

I started thinking, if he is alive then I can be raised from the dead and live forever too. Eternal life became a reality to me on that day and I have been loving and serving Jesus ever since.

Joni Gilbertsen
New Castle, Pa.

"Truly I tell you, unless you change and become like little children, you will never enter the kingdom of heaven." Matthew 18:3 (NIV)

Making Plans and Taking Steps

I began preaching when I was twenty years old in a little church in Neapolis, Ohio. I married Marilyn that same year. The two of us thought we would stay in that town all of our lives.

In 1964, the Elders from North Highlands Church of Christ on Archer Avenue in Fort Wayne, were determined that we were to come to their church. We prayed over it and felt God's call, so we moved to Fort Wayne.

The Church flourished and grew and helped spawn Christ Church in Georgetown. We soon outgrew our building so we made plans to build a million dollar building in North Highlands community, a suburb of Fort Wayne. A bank promised financing, we had plans drawn and we held a ground breaking ceremony with the mayor present. There was even a picture in the newspaper and a contractor on site.

That year, 1973, there was a severe downturn in the economy. When we went to the bank to obtain our loan for $800,000 we were told the money was no longer available. What do you do? We had made plans and promises. What was God thinking? What did God want us to do?

I said, "We are going to prayer." I had heard about early morning praying in Korea. I said, "we're going to go to prayer at 5:30 in the morning. and we're going to pray until we get an answer."

That went on for six weeks. Do you know how early 5:30 in the morning is when you start praying at that hour for six weeks, seven mornings a week? I'm a morning person but I was never consistently up that early and going to bed later every night.

One morning following prayer, I was with a group of pastors who heard the mayor of our city, Ivan Lebamoff, speak and challenge each of us to look at the downtown area of Fort Wayne, where it seemed everyone was leaving in 1973. The mayor urged us to look at the downtown as a place of potential and opportunity.

God laid it on my heart to remember the empty church building at the corner of Broadway and Wayne, which had been the Wayne Street Methodist Church. After breakfast, I went to that building, opened the door and I couldn't believe what I saw.

There before me was the exact floor plan we were proposing to build and still intact since1871. It was constructed of sturdy oak, had stained glass windows, a pipe organ,, a wood floor gymnasium, a commercial kitchen and a large sanctuary.

For two hours I walked around in there with disbelief sparring with God. This can't be and how can we do this? I went home and I couldn't speak. Marilyn thought I had been in some sort of accident.

That night as Marilyn and I walked, I said, "Honey, I've dreamed a dream or seen a vision."

After I shared with her my amazing discovery, she said, "Bob I told you two weeks ago we should buy that building when we went past it." I hadn't heard her but God did and the Broadway Christian Church was born.

About eighty families, approximately 300 people, came with us from the suburbs to the city. Interestingly. most of the people who came with us were those who came to Christ during my nine years at North Highlands.

Our first service at Broadway Christian was January 6, 1974.

I began preaching on discipleship and what it means to seriously follow Jesus. I spoke several consecutive Sundays on repentance.

On one occasion, our Church School Superintendent came forward, with his wife at his side, weeping and confessed he was a closet alcoholic. His Sunday School Class, with an elder leading them, surrounded him and vowed to stay with him. That morning was a watershed spiritually for the people knew then it was a safe place to confess their sins.

I am now retired from Broadway Christian but I look back over those 28 years, and I marvel at what God did, not only through the growth in numbers, (2,000 people attending five worship services in two locations,) but also the churches and organizations that were birthed out of Broadway.

It is obvious what happened in 1973 when the bank didn't give us the promised funds. God saved us from ourselves.

Pastor BobYawberg
Fort Wayne, IN.

"A man's heart devises his way, but the Lord directs his steps." (Proverbs 16:9)

Epilogue

This compilation of God stories in America had its genesis in 1986. On the Thursday before Labor Day weekend, I had invited my youngest son, then 18, to my house for dinner. His mother, (we were recently divorced) graciously let him borrow her car, as he didn't want to ride over on his Harley in the rain.

We chatted freely over one of his favorite meals, lasagna. He told me for the Labor Day weekend he was going to Vermont with his friend Doug and Doug's family. They had recently had a ski lodge built in Andover, Vermont.

When it was time for him to leave, he stood in my small kitchen with a satisfying smile on his face. He handed me a fifty dollar bill. It was the final payment on a loan I had given him for something, maybe the Harley.

We hugged, and as we did I realized this tow head was no longer a boy but a strong young man. I stood in the open doorway when he left and waved. He tooted the horn as he drove off. As I watched the tail lights disappear down the street, I had an overwhelming feeling I was going to remember this moment for the rest of my life.

On Labor Day, I was visiting a friend in Pennsylvania when I received a call that Steven had died in the loft of that ski lodge when it caught fire. His best friend's family all escaped.

The world stopped for me. I felt like I had been kicked in the stomach and hit over the head at the same time. On the return flight to Hartford, I sat in the plane, my mind in a daze. The next few days are a blur. There was a memorial service and Steven's mother and I cried uncontrollably from the same pew, with our daughter and older son between us.

Two nights later, I was alone at home trying to write thank you notes to friends for their expressions of sympathy. I was overcome with grief and fell to my knees and I cried out, "Lord, I can't handle this. I need your help!"

I heard a voice say, "I'm right here."

The voice was so clear that I opened my eyes and looked around the room. That was the moment God became real to me. That night the Lord comforted this hurting soul, "with the peace that passes all understanding."

After this experience, I began to see God's hand everywhere. Although I had "done" church most of my adult life, I didn't have a relationship with God.

Someone suggested I attend a men's breakfast downtown. The facilitator of the breakfast was C.B. Nagel, a staffer with Campus Crusade for Christ. He met with me, one-on-one, for several weeks and showed me how I could have a personal relationship with God by asking Jesus into my life as my Lord and Savior. Even though I attended many churches over the years, I never understood how I could know God personally.

Once I invited Jesus into my life, I felt less stress and more peace. I began reading the Bible daily and attending a Bible preaching church.

I began to share my spiritual experience with other people, and many shared theirs with me, and so God Stories in America was born.

These experiences are from people like you. It could be a friend, a loved one, or a kid next door. My prayer is these events, which God orchestrated, will encourage you, inspire you and renew your faith.

Don't know God personally? You can begin by asking God into your life. Don't wait, do it now. Then find a loving, Bible-preaching church, and associate with other **believers.**

Blessings, RMS

"For everyone that asks, receives;
and he that seeks, finds; and to
him that knocks it shall be
opened." Matthew (7:8)

To the younger generation:

"Make God your GPS
You will love the journey."
(Anonymous)

What is Your God Story?

Do you have a God experience that you are willing to share with others in a future edition of God Stories in America to advance His Kingdom?

Tell us, in your own words, about your experience, and when it is published, you will be sent a complimentary copy of the publication containing your submission.

Your story can be up to 1500 words, must be an actual event you experienced or witnessed and written by you or someone you authorize.

E-mail your God experience to the address below, and be sure to put God Story in the subject line. Include your name, your hometown and state and where the experience happened if not obvious from your narrative.

E-mail your narrative to:

godstoriesinamerica@gmail.com

If you have questions call us at 941-400-3109

R. Malcolm Salter, Editor